Music in Japan

Music in Japan

∞

EXPERIENCING MUSIC,
EXPRESSING CULTURE

∞

BONNIE C. WADE

New York   Oxford
Oxford University Press
2005

Oxford University Press

Oxford   New York
Auckland   Bangkok   Buenos Aires   Cape Town   Chennai
Dar es Salaam   Delhi   Hong Kong   Istanbul   Karachi   Kolkata
Kuala Lumpur   Madrid   Melbourne   Mexico City   Mumbai
Nairobi   São Paulo   Shanghai   Taipei   Tokyo   Toronto

Published by Oxford University Press, Inc.
198 Madison Avenue, New York, New York, 10016
www.oup.com

Oxford is a registered trademark of Oxford University Press

Library of Congress Cataloging-in-Publication Data
Wade, Bonnie C.
    Music in Japan : experiencing music, expressing culture / Bonnie C. Wade.
        p. cm. — (Global music series)
    Includes bibliographical references and index.
    ISBN 0-19-514487-2 — ISBN 0-19-514488-0 (pbk.)
        1. Music—Japan—History and criticism. 2. Music—Japan—Foreign influences.
I. Title. II. Series.

ML340.W22 2004
780′.952—dc22

                                                                                2004041486

Cover image: The Yoshida Brothers in concert. So fast is the virtuosic playing in
their Tsugaru syamisen-pop music style (CD track 14) that the plectrum is blurred
in this photo.

Printing number: 9 8 7 6 5 4 3 2 1

Printed in the United States of America
on acid-free paper

GLOBAL MUSIC SERIES

General Editors: Bonnie C. Wade and Patricia Shehan Campbell

Music in East Africa, Gregory Barz
Music in Central Java, Benjamin Brinner
Teaching Music Globally, Patricia Shehan Campbell
Carnival Music in Trinidad, Shannon Dudley
Music in Bali, Lisa Gold
Music in Ireland, Dorothea E. Hast and Stanley Scott
Music in the Middle East, Scott Marcus
Music in Brazil, John Patrick Murphy
Music in America, Adelaida Reyes
Music in Bulgaria, Timothy Rice
Music in North India, George E. Ruckert
Mariachi Music in America, Daniel Sheehy
Music in West Africa, Ruth M. Stone
Music in South India, T. Viswanathan and Matthew Harp Allen
Music in Japan, Bonnie C. Wade
Thinking Musically, Bonnie C. Wade
Music in China, J. Lawrence Witzleben

Contents

∞

Foreword

∞

In the past three decades interest in music around the world has surged, as evidenced in the proliferation of courses at the college level, the burgeoning "world music" market in the recording business, and the extent to which musical performance is evoked as a lure in the international tourist industry. This heightened interest has encouraged an explosion in ethnomusicological research and publication, including the production of reference works and textbooks. The original model for the "world music" course—if this is Tuesday, this must be Japan—has grown old, as has the format of textbooks for it, either a series of articles in single multiauthored volumes that subscribe to the idea of "a survey" and have created a canon of cultures for study, or single-authored studies purporting to cover world musics or ethnomusicology. The time has come for a change.

This Global Music Series offers a new paradigm. Teachers can now design their own courses; choosing from a set of case study volumes, they can decide which and how many musics they will cover. The series also does something else; rather than uniformly taking a large region and giving superficial examples from several different countries within it, in some case studies authors have focused on a specific culture or a few countries within a larger region. Its length and approach permits each volume greater depth than the usual survey. Themes significant in each volume guide the choice of music that is discussed. The contemporary musical situation is the point of departure in all the volumes, with historical information and traditions covered as they elucidate the present. In addition, a set of unifying topics such as gender, globalization, and authenticity occur throughout the series. These are addressed in the framing volume, *Thinking Musically*, which sets the stage for the case studies by introducing ways to think about how people make music meaningful and useful in their lives and presenting basic musical concepts as they are practiced in musical systems around the world. A second framing volume, *Teaching Music Globally*, guides teachers in the use of *Thinking Musically* and the case studies.

The series subtitle, "Experiencing Music, Expressing Culture," also puts in the forefront the people who make music or in some other way experience it and also through it express shared culture. This resonance with global history studies, with their focus on processes and themes that permit cross-study, occasions the title of this Global Music Series.

Bonnie C. Wade
Patricia Shehan Campbell
General Editors

Preface

∽

With an understanding of contemporary musical life in Japan as the primary aim of this volume, I shall travel between the present day and history. Three themes provide the focus and guide the selection of music on the accompanying CD: (1) the interface of Japan with other cultures, (2) the gradual process of popularization that has occurred in the musical arts throughout Japanese history, and (3) intertextuality in Japanese arts.

Music in Japan has been profoundly affected by interface with others, by both the Asian (continental and island) and European cultural spheres (Europe and the Americas). The nature of the interface has been shaped by a process of learning from other cultures, followed by assimilation and indigenization of ideas and items. Unlike most ethnomusicological work on Japan, this text embraces the reality that the Japanese term for music, *ongaku*, is now used to refer to music in the Western tradition or by composers trained in Western music rather than in the Japanese tradition. Music for Japanese instruments is categorized apart, as *hōgaku*, when that music has been transmitted through time or newly composed by musicians in the traditional sphere. In chapter 1 I consider the international interface that occurred when Japan looked to powerful Western nations to modernize rapidly. In chapter 2 I focus on Japan's importation of music from China, Korea, and other parts of Asia in the first millennium.

In chapter 3 I address the results of international interface with a focus on musical developments within Japan. The booming industry in popular music today, while inseparable from Japan's technological and commercial leadership as well as ubiquitous importation of foreign culture, is a contemporary form of a fundamentally important aspect of Japanese musical culture through time: a gradual process of popularization by which a local or a group's music becomes accessible to a broader range of people. In chapter 3 illustrations of gradual popularization range from ancient court music staged alongside new popular music, the elite *koto* of court music as it became the favored chamber music instrument, Tsugaru *syamisen* (*shamisen*) music turned into a popular rage, *syakuhati* (*shakuhachi*) music beyond the temples of the Fuke Zen Buddhist sect, and others.

Intertextuality is at the heart of the Japanese performing arts, as familiar themes and musical material, sounds, and structures are maintained but transformed in ever fresh ways, serving to keep cultural memory alive (chapters 4 and 5). In chapter 4 I trace a story introduced in chapter 3 as it is performed in the styles of fifteenth-century *nō* theater, nineteenth-century *kabuki* theater, and in more detail, in a 1945 film by Akira Kurosawa. In chapter 5 intertextuality reappears in several ways—in jazz, where authenticity is an issue, and in contemporary classical music. In chapter 5 I return to the themes of international interface and intertextuality to demonstrate how they are ongoing. I end in chapter 6 with a consideration of contributions Japan is now making to music in the world.

I make three other points about the book. One is that I have been willfully inconsistent, using both the Kunrei system of transliteration (*syakuhati* for *shakuhachi*, *syamisen* for *shamisen*) and the Hepburn in order to acknowledge both the preferences of Japanese scholars and familiar practice. Another is that the cost of reproducing selections from Japanese recording companies, particularly regarding popular music, is usually quite prohibitive, and that has determined the items and length of them used in this book. Finally, I spell the names of Japanese first name first, last name last, as opposed to the Japanese system of putting the last name first, so as to not confuse matters for Western readers.

This book is the result of more than forty years of experience with music in Japan. When I first traveled there, fresh out of college and looking for adventure, I earned living expenses by teaching emergency English to firemen in Tokyo before the 1964 Olympics. Thus I could afford to spend a wonderful year studying *koto* intensively with Yori Kishibe, of whom I always think with appreciation. I have continued study and research since then, returning frequently to Japan, and have regularly taught Japanese music (and given instruction in *koto*) first at Brown University and, since 1976, at the University of California, Berkeley. While I have always been drawn to Japan's traditional musical sphere, as an ethnomusicologist I have been equally intrigued by its contemporary music world, not only of composed classical music but also the rich popular music scene. I hope that in this book my enthusiasm for that country's rich and diverse arts will help you enjoy your musical journey to Japan.

I wish to acknowledge many people. In Japan these include my family, the Nakajimas, who through decades of friendship have given so generously of themselves in my scholarly endeavors; my very able research assistants Tokiko Inoue and Fukiko Shinohara; Kimiko Shimbo of the Japan Federation of Composers for years of advice and help in the contemporary composition world; my colleagues Osamu Yamaguti, for his advice and friendship through the years, and Yosihiko Tokumaru; Yoshiko Okazaki, Tatsuko Takizawa, and Kiyoko Motegi for their generosity and connections for notations, for *nukui-bayashi* materials, and for photographs of instruments, respectively; Kiyotomi Yoshizaki for insights on *SupaKabuki*; Catherine Ochi of the Drum Museum; Shuhei Hosokawa with his expertise on the popular music scene and for drawing my attention to Kurosawa's film; Koji Satoh of Tenri University for his generosity with *gagaku* materials; Akira Tanaka of Zen-on, Nanako Ikefuji of Schott, Takeshi Inoue and Kenji Okazaki of King Records, Makiko Kawai of Japan Victor, Akira Matsuda of Fontec, and Hiroshi Isaka of Camerata, for their help with permissions and materials; Yukio Kojima of Kojima and ALM recordings for his excellent recording of the *Ataka* play; the Kita Nogakudo actors and musicians who gave of their time for performance recordings: Sadamu Omura, Shingo Kō, Mitsuo Kama, Daisaku Tani, and Shinya Inoue; Michio Takemori of the Tokyo Metropolitan Symphony Orchestra, Maestro Hiroyuki Iwaki of the Kanagawa Orchestra, and Kenji Yanai of the National Theater; the Nakada family, Mikio Itoh, and Kazuhiko Arimoto of Pony Canyon for their generosity on the "Chiisai mitsuketa" recording; Keiko Abe and Motoko Kobayashi for Abe's marimba music; Shigetoshi Nagamine of the Historiographical Institute Library at the University of Tokyo and Shigeru Miyakawa for facilitating graphic materials; and the artist Hotsuka Toyokuni.

Among the community of longtime residents of Japan, the following colleagues have been generous with their time, knowledge, and expertise: Rick Emmert, of the Kita Nohgakudo, for video recording and notation of *Ataka* excerpts; John Lytton, for the *nagauta* drumming transcription of *Kanjinchō*: Christopher Yohmei Blasdel (*syakuhati*), Mark Oshima (*kiyomoto*), and Steven Nelson (*gagaku*) in their spheres of expertise. Steve McClure, Philip Brasor, and especially Mark Schilling were of great assistance with their knowledge of the various Japanese media. David Hopkins was very helpful about permissions, as was Judith Herd, whom I wish to thank for her years of insightful help on the contemporary music scene. Although they are not residents, when I intersected in Japan with Jennifer Milioto, she introduced me to the underground pop music scene, and Ian Condry and I exchanged good discussions on Japanese popular music. Lyn Matsuoka, a renowned *kabuki* artist, provided a wonderful apartment in Tokyo that greatly enhanced my ability to undertake my research.

I also thank here just a few of my many Japanese composer friends who write wonderful music and have been enormously generous with me for this book: Akira Nishimura, Tokuhide Niimi, Somei Satoh, Toshio Hosokawa, Akira Ifukube, Mica Nozawa, and Yuji Takahashi. I am especially indebted to Minoru Miki for years of friendship and help with recordings and permissions. And I particularly want to thank Joji Yuasa and Keiko Fujiie for their friendship and for allowing me to reproduce some of their beautiful music.

Among Japan's great musical performers I am grateful to Keiko Abe for her wonderful marimbas and music she has written for them and on which she is an artist nonpareil. And most particularly, I want to thank my dear, longtime friend Keiko Nosaka for her innumerable kindnesses, help, fantastic music, and willingness and ability to push the boundaries and to bridge the traditional and contemporary *koto* worlds in incomparable fashion.

Outside Japan I have benefited from colleagues and friends Allan Marett, William Malm, Luciana Galliano, Mari Ono and Yuki Miura of Music from Japan, Cathy Carapella of Diamond Time, Taylor Atkins, and Michael Peluse. I also thank my author colleagues in the GMS Series; Victor Fung, the educational consultant who has worked with me on the educational website materials; Pat Campbell, my co-general editor; and executive editor Jan Beatty, assistant editor Talia Krohn, and project editor Lisa Grzan of Oxford University Press.

Finally, here in my university I thank the Center for Japanese Studies for generous research support under its chairs Mary Elizabeth Berry, Andrew Barshay, and Steven Vogel, and assistant Keiko Hjersmann; James Coates, our able staff person in the Department of Music, graduate students Philip Flavin, for discussions about Japanese music, and Eliot Bates, for mastering the CD; and the late Jerry and Evelyn Hemmings Chambers for endowing the chair which I have held and that has helped underwrite these endeavors.

Last, but definitely not least, has been the enormous help on this project of three fantastic research assistants, all graduate students here: Adam Steckler, Group in Asian Studies, for his work on databases, *man-*

gas, and *animé*; Janice Kande, Department of East Asian Languages and Cultures, for translations and cultural insights; and Marié Abe, Department of Music, for translations, insights into the younger generation scene, and particularly on cutting-edge Japanese popular music.

To all of the above, and many more along the way too numerous to mention, I am deeply indebted, especially the marvelous music makers of Japan.

CD Track List

∞

1. Antonio Vivaldi, "The Four Seasons: Summer," excerpt. Yasuko Ohtani and Kazuyoshi Akiyama (violin). Sony Records SRCR. C. 1986, 1997.
2. Joji Yuasa, "Scenes from Basho." From *Eye on Genesis: Orchestral Works by Joji Yuasa*. Contemporary Composers from Japan series. Hiroyuki Iwaki, conductor, Tokyo Metropolitan Symphony Orchestra. Fontec FOCD 2508. c. 1986. Courtesy of Zen-On, Fontec, Hiroyuki Iwaki, and the Tokyo Metropolitan Symphony Orchestra.
3. *Nō: Ataka: Ha* sixth *dan* from "Ika ni Benkei." Sadamu Omura (*shite*), Daisaku Tani (*waki*), Shinya Inoue (*kokata*), Mitsuo Kama (*ō-tsuzumi*), Shingo Ko (*ko-tsuzumi*), Richard Emmert (*nōkan*). Recorded for the author at Kita Nogakudo, Tokyo by Yukio Kojima, 8 May 2002.
4. Ludwig van Beethoven, Symphony No. 9 in D Minor, Op. 125, finale, excerpt. Universal Recording Factory, URFC 0033. Nagaoka Daiku Chorus and Fuji Beethoven Chorus. Chorus Conductor: Akiyasu Fukushima. Conductor: Koho Uno. Ensemble Sakura. Baritone: Makoto Narita. Live recording: 1 July 2001. Tokorozawa Civic Cultural Center "Muse" [Ark Hall], Tokorozawa, Japan. c. 2001.
5. "Nasori." From *Gagaku (Court Music)*, excerpt. Music Department, Imperial Household, Tokyo. C. 59, 2 Columbia CL 69. c. 1959.
6. "Rokudan." Shinichi Yuize. From *The Japanese Koto: Shinichi Yuize*. Cook Laboratories (Stamford, Conn.), Cook 1132, n.d. Courtesy of the Smithsonian Institution.
7. "Sanja matsuri" (*Tokiwazu*), excerpt. From *1000 Years of Japanese Classical Music* (Nihon Koten Ongaku Taikei), vol. 7. Kodansha 686161. c. 1980–82.
8. "Netori banshiki." From *Gagaku (Togaku)*. *Gagaku* Music Society of Tenri University, Japan. TDR 163–4. c. 2000. Courtesy of Koji Satoh, Director, *Gagaku* Music Society of Tenri University.

9. "Chōshi ichikotsu-chō" (*bugaku* style), excerpt. From *Gagaku: Shunnoden* (*Song of the Nightingale*). Shigenkai Court *Gagaku* Orchestra. Japan Victor JVC SJL-57. c. 1973.

10. "Etenraku banshiki-chō." From *Gagaku* (*Togaku*). *Gagaku* Music Society of Tenri University, Japan. TDR 163–4. c. 2000. Courtesy of Koji Satoh, Director, *Gagaku* Music Society of Tenri University.

11. "November Steps," excerpt. From *Requiem for Strings, November Steps, Far calls, coming, far!* Nippon Columbia. CO-79441 Devon. 1992.

12. "Koku reibo." From *A Bell Ringing in the Empty Sky: Japanese Shakuhachi Music*. Goro Yamaguchi (*syakuhati*). Nonesuch. H-72025. [1968]. Courtesy of Warner Atlantic.

13. "Yaegoromo," excerpt. From *Japan Jiuta*. Yonin no Kai Ensemble (Tokyo). Ocora C 580069. c.1998.

14. "Ibuki" (Tsugaru *syamisen*), excerpt. From *Ibuki: Ryoichiro Yoshida and Kenichi Yoshida*. Victor VZCG-161. c. 1999.

15. *Kanjinchō*. Part 10. Live recording at Minami-za in Kyoto (12, 13 December 1985). Danjuro Ichikawa, Takao Kataoka, Senjaku Nakamura, and others. King Records KICH 2003. c. 1990. Courtesy of King Records.

16. "Yumigahana," excerpt. From *Ondekoza*. Victor VDRY-28006. c. 1989.

17. "Nukui bayashi" (Meguro style *matsuri bayashi*). Nukuibayashi Preservation Society. Excerpt from "Yatai." Private CD. n.d. Courtesy of Toshio Osawa.

18. Minoru Miki, "Tennyō" for twenty-stringed *koto* solo. Keiko Nosaka (*koto*). Camerata CMT-1018. c. 1979. Courtesy of Camerata and Zen-on.

19. Seventeen-string *koto*, excerpt. From *Shinichi Yuize: Preludes for Koto*. Yasuko Nakashima (*koto*). CBS/Sony 50 AG 609. c.1979.

20. Michio Miyagi, "Haru no umi." Victor Japan LR 520, c.1958. Courtesy of Japan Victor and the Miyagi Michio Kinenkan.

21. *Nō: Ataka. Ha* fifth *dan*, from "Hōgan-dono." See CD track 3.

22. *Nō: Ataka. Kyū dan* from "Geni geni." See CD track 3.

23. Spoken *Ataka no mai*. Drummed *Ataka no mai*. See CD track 3.

24. "Hagoromo,"excerpt. Nippon Columbia PLP 20, n.d.

25. *Kanjinchō*. Part 9. See CD track 15.

26. *Kanjinchō*. Part 5. See CD track 15.

27. *Kanjinchō*. Part 2. See CD track 15.

28. *Kanjinchō*. Part 12 from "Geni, geni." See CD track 15.

29. *Kanjinchō*. Part 12 from *Ataka no mai*. See CD track 15.

30. Men's chorus from *Men Who Step on the Tiger's Tail*, excerpt. From *The Complete Sound Tracks of Akira Kurosawa*, vol. 1. Fun House FHCF-1134, [1946].
31. Sugii Koichi, "Yagi bushi," excerpt. From *A History of King Jazz Recordings: Pioneers of Japanese Jazz I*. King Novelty Orchestra. King 9031. c. 1991.
32. Akira Nishimura, "Ketiak" (1979). From *Ketiak: Works of Akira Nishimura*. Performed by Percussion-Group 72. Camerata 32CM-89. c. 1988. Courtesy of Zen-On and Camerata.
33. *Kecak Bonasari of Bali, Monkey Dance*, excerpt, track 1. Maharani. c. 1991.
34. "Salsa no tiene frontera," excerpt. Written by Nora. Arranged by Orquesta de la Luz and Sergio George. BMG Funhouse BVCK 37065. c. 2000.
35. "Tokyo Tokyo," excerpt. From *ECD Presents the original Motion Picture "Thumpin' Camp."* K-Dub Shine and DJ Kensei. Cutting Edge ECD CTCR-14048. c. 1996.
36. Keiko Fujiie, "Ten no yō na chi, soshite chi no yō na ten." ("Like heaven, earth, so like earth, heaven"). Recorded live at the premiere performance by Reigakusha at the National Theatre, Tokyo. c. 1999. By permission of the National Theatre of Japan.
37. Yoshinao Nakada, "Chiisai aki mitsuketa." Pony Canyon PCCG-00447. c. 1998. Courtesy of the Yoshinao Nakada family and Pony Canyon.
38. Toshio Hosokawa, "Singing Trees: Requiem for Toru Takemitsu," excerpt. For children's chorus (1996). From *Works by Toshio Hosokawa*. The Little Singers of Tokyo. Saeko Hasegawa, conductor. Fontec FOCD 3441. c. 1997.
39. Tokuhide Niimi, Symphony no. 2 for Orchestra and Mixed Chorus," excerpt. From *Min-On Contemporary Music Festival 1986*. Osaka Philharmonic Chorus and Kyoto Echo Chorus. Choral Conductor Kenichi Asai. Osaka Philharmonic Orchestra, Tadaaki Otaka, conductor. Camerata 32 CM-298. c. 1993.
40. "Sakura no uta" ("Song of the cherry blossoms"), excerpt. From *Misora Hibari Compilation 2000: Kawa no nagare no yo ni 2000*. Columbia COCP-31053. c. 2000.
41. "Kotonoha," excerpt. From *Koto no ha*. Hajime Chitose. Augusta Records TGCS-1190. c. 2001.
42. "Peace!," excerpt. From *SmapVest*. Music Face 2 FAKE. Arranged Nagaoka. Chorus: Oh! Be, Takamoto Nozawa. Victor VICL-60726. c. 2001.

43. "Ano natsu no mama de," excerpt. Lyrics by Misia. Music by Hidetoshi Yamada. Arranged by Akihisa Matsuura. From Misia Marvelous BMG. BVCS-21022 C. 2001.
44. "Distance" excerpt. From *Distance*. Utada Hikaru. Toshiba-EMI TOCT-24601. c. 2001.
45. "Riding on the Rocket," excerpt. From *Let's Knife*. Shonen Knife. Words and music by Naoko Yamano. MCA Victor, MVCD-3. c. 1992.
46. "24/7," excerpt. From *Monkey Girl Odyssey*. Dreams Come True. Toshiba EMI TOCT-56005. c. 2001.
47. "Shanddraviza," excerpt. From *Tzomvorgha*. Ruins. Maigabutsu MGC-22. c. 2002.
48. "Super Are You," excerpt. From *Super Ae*. Boredoms. Warner Music, Japan WPC6-8442. c. 1998.
49. "*Sabu to ichi to torimono-hikae*, Opening Theme," excerpt. From *Otomo Yoshide Plays the Music of Takeo Yamashita*. Otomo Yoshide. P-Vine Records PCD-5804. c. 1999.
50. Toshiko Akiyoshi, "Kogun," excerpt. From *The Best of Toshiko Akiyoshi*. Toshiko Akiyoshi/Lew Tabachin Big Band. BVCJ 37299 (BMG). c. 2002.
51. Keiko Abe, "Dream of Cherry Blossoms." From *Marimba Fantasy: The Art of Keiko Abe*. Keiko Abe (marimba). Xebec XECC-1004. 1998. Courtesy of Xebec Music Publishing Co., Ltd.

CHAPTER 1

International Interface: Looking Westward

∞

SETTING THE SCENE

April is turning into May and, alas, the brief but intense national period of relishing the cherry blossoms has passed. But never fear: any reason to "do" a festival will suffice. Streaming into the subways, trains, and buses of an incredible public transportation system, then out to myriad public spaces, what seems to be a large percentage of metropolitan Tokyo's 18 million people turns out for a nearly week-long celebration of the start of the spring season. I head for the city's Harajuku area where, it seems to me, much of the history of modern Japan comes together (figure 1.1).

Beside riotously decorated storefronts across the street from the train station, barkers for the teen-oriented shops and eateries call out boisterously. To the right of the station, the sidewalk leads people of all ages up a short rise toward Yoyogi Park. At the crest to the right, literally bridging the Harajuku area and the park, a wide path—that is, a road that becomes a path on Sundays and holidays—crosses over the railroad tracks. This is Hokoten, "pedestrian's paradise," which for over twenty years has been a gathering spot for bands taking a first step to fame (figure 1.2) and for small clusters of teens preening in *kosu pure* (costume play), having donned the dress of their favorite pop idol or character in a *manga* (comic book) or just anything fantastic they wish (figure 1.3).

From Hokoten, Japan's history can be seen in a sweep. Tall contemporary buildings with walls of glass reflect the congested commercial area, the crowded city streets and sidewalks, and somewhat worn stadiums built for the 1964 Tokyo Olympics. In the distance rises the NHK building, center of the powerful government-supported broadcasting

1

FIGURE 1.1 *Maps of Japan and Japan in the context of Asia.*

FIGURE 1.2 *An aspiring trio, Third Time Trick, there early to get a good spot on Hokoten, the pedestrian bridge at Harajuku in Tokyo.* *(Photo by the author.)*

system and home to a major concert hall for orchestras and other Europe-derived ensembles (CD tracks 1 and 2). Also nearby is the National Nō Theater, designed specifically for productions of *nō*, the musico-dramatic genre developed for the elite *samurai* (warrior) class in the fifteenth century (CD track 3). Down a side street is the *ukiyo-e* museum that houses woodblock prints by artists who documented the vitality of the urban popular entertainment industry from the seventeenth century (figure 1.4). As well, a broad, carefully groomed pathway shows the way to the Meiji Shrine.

The Meiji Shrine celebrates Japan's modernization, commemorating the emperor and the period (1868–1912) when the government officially turned to the West for ideas that would end hundreds of years of relative isolation and catapult Japan onto the world stage. For the spring festival, a raised stage has been erected in the inner courtyard of the inner shrine. In a packed week of events, highly ritualized performances of *nō* drama and *kyōgen* comic plays will be offered free of charge, along with performances of a variety of traditional musical genres and demonstrations of martial arts and other forms of traditional Japanese culture.

FIGURE 1.3   Kosu pure *(costume play)* at Harajuku, spring 2002.   *(Photo by the author.)*

Even as performances proceed, traditional-style Shinto weddings—one after the other—take place within the shrine, having been scheduled long in advance for this auspicious time and meaningful place (figure 1.5). Each ends in a formal, quiet procession of the wedding party through the shrine grounds past the rear of the audience, which is there for a performance and grants the families privacy by discreetly ignoring them. Outside, the shrine path provides access to the private Harajuku railway station for the imperial family, who are significant even in democratic Japan. Another path leads to the rest of Yoyogi Park, where spacious grounds host picnicking, dancing to boom boxes, singing of traditional folk songs or contemporary tunes with friends,

FIGURE 1.4   Syakuhati *in* ukiyo-e *woodblock print in the author's collection.*
Kabuki actor Kodanji Ichikawa.   *(Print by Kunichika, published 1864.)*

throwing baseballs and Frisbees, or eating at one of the many stands
erected for the occasion.

The start of the spring season occasions many festivals (*matsuri*), most
of which impart a sense of the local, even in the huge metropolitan areas. From a flyer distributed at the Japan National Tourist Office's
Tourist Information Center in Tokyo, I discovered the Kanamura *matsuri* in Kawasaki, a suburb about an hour by train from the city center.
There, contemporary life meets tradition, as described in the flyer:

> This festival traces its origins to the Edo period, when Kawasaki's
> ladies of the night prayed for success in their business and protection

FIGURE 1.5 Shō, hichiriki, *and* ryūteki *played by musicians for a wedding at a Tokyo shrine.* *(Photo by the author.)*

from syphilis. At cherry blossom time they would gather baskets of bamboo shoots and other spring delicacies, carry the shrine's phallic image in procession through the streets, and then sit down on mats spread in the shrine courtyard to enjoy a merry banquet.

Now the participants have changed to the general public, the foods consumed have become international, and the sexual ailment most on people's minds is AIDS. But in joining together to celebrate the advent of spring, people today maintain a close connection with their roots.

So welcome. Whether your prayers be for success in business, a fertile marriage, wedded bliss, healthy progeny, an easy delivery, or personal good health, the Kanamura Shrine is still the focus of the faith of the community, as it has been for centuries.

And if your beliefs do not allow you to pray in the Japanese fashion, we hope you will still give generously to support our campaign to alleviate the plight of sufferers from HIV and AIDS.

The festival begins on Saturday evening with the fashioning of symbolic figures from rice paste, followed by *karaoke* singing and food. The next morning, rituals are enacted by a chief priest, with the participation of community leaders and other dignitaries. The ceremonies close with a toast of *omiki*, sacred *sake* (rice wine). Close to noon, attention turns to portable shrines (*o-mikoshi*), each imbued with the spirit of Kanamura-sama, the shrine deity. After blessings, each shrine is hoisted and carried, palanquin-style with rods over the shoulder, in a rambunctious procession through the neighborhood. The hardworking, cheerful group of men shout "*Washoi, washoi*," to coordinate their forward motion. All will be ready for the food and drink, *karaoke*, and dance that will end the day.

As you can see already, musical culture in Japan is a rich and varied potpourri, resulting from more than a millennium and a half of interface with cultures beyond its island shores. The nature of that interface has been shaped by a uniquely Japanese process of borrowing, then assimilating, the foreign. In comparison to countries such as the United States, the population of Japan's islands has always been relatively homogeneous; whereas most countries achieve their cultural diversity as a result of people migrating in, Japan has achieved its musical diversity by seeking it elsewhere. I have devoted this chapter and the next specifically to discussing when, why, and how musics of other cultures came to be a part of Japanese life. I pick this theme up again in chapter 5. The stories are often told but bear repeating in order to contextualize music at the present time.

"THE WEST" GOES TO JAPAN

∞

Dear Bonnie,

Here at last! I have written down what I rattled on to you about in conversation. My husband and I spent Christmas of 1996 in Japan with our old friends Hiro and Yoshiko. They invited us to a Christmas music performance in Tokyo; Yoshiko would be playing cello in a string quartet. Many amateurs, individuals and groups, would be taking part in this performance, an event that I believe takes place yearly.

In 1996 the performance took place at a German restaurant that was reserved for the afternoon. It is, in all seasons, but particularly during the Christmas season, decorated to reflect the basic "Bavarian Christmas card scene" that has been adopted everywhere since Victoria first caused a pine tree to be dragged into the palace. There is a stage visible from all the tables that is large enough for up to 30 people to stand up there and sing. There is a Christmas theme to it all, but it is obvious that some favorite songs are put in there anyway because everyone likes them and knows them. Pachelbel and Verdi were by no means slighted. There were barbershop quartets, string quartets, and big groups that are virtual glee clubs. About fifteen groups (perhaps as many as twenty), many of whom have been singing or playing together for most of their adult lives, rehearse for this event for months. There was no Japanese music of any kind.

Well over a hundred people participate; at least an equal number of relatives and friends attend. Everyone is very convivial and applauds everyone else madly, except in some cases their own close relatives. Hiro turned to us, as Yoshiko was hauling her cello onstage, and whispered that he wished to apologize for his wife's terrible playing of the cello. He was, of course, immensely proud of her. She played perfectly, then came to sit beside us. "I was so terrible, terrible! I apologize for bringing you to hear my terrible playing!" And so on.

Need I add that the whole affair ends with the chorale from Beethoven's Ninth [CD track 4], which includes the entire audience? I was so glad that I knew the words. As you know, they ALL do. We were clearly being exposed to a genre all of its own, with meanings I could only imagine, but not fully understand.

Susan [Kepner]
March 7, 2002

∞

At the end of year, concert performances of the Ninth are held everywhere, and many amateur singers look forward to singing in these choruses. This can probably be considered a phenomenon peculiar to Japan. (Inoue, Ozawa, Sakon, and Hosaka, 1996).

Contact between Japan and Europe began when nations and mercantile companies sent traders to the islands in the sixteenth century.

Soldiers were on board ready to defend them, and often missionaries intent on the spread of their particular brands of European cultures. Japan's first experience with Western music came with music for their worship. Seeing potential encroachment of foreign ideas that threatened political control, Japanese leaders responded for the most part with policies of restrictions and constraints to control the nature and extent of relationships. For instance, Christianity was banned in 1588.

In the Tokugawa period (1600–1868) Japan's official governmental policy was one of nearly complete isolation: for about 250 years Japan turned mostly inward, a feudal society more or less unto itself. Its ancient imperial household languished without political power in Kyoto, the cultural and spiritual center located in the western region (*kansai*) of the main island (Honshu). The locus of political and economic power was the burgeoning city of Edo in the east (*kantō*), home of the ruling Tokugawa family with the *shōgun* at its head. As a result of the isolation, European music was almost entirely extinguished.

However, with European, British, and also American presence ever more insistent as the system of global colonialism threatened the independence of more and more of the world's peoples, isolation became increasingly difficult to sustain. On the evening of 8 July 1853 Captain Matthew Perry, commander in chief of the U.S. naval forces stationed in the East India, China, and Japan Seas, sailed into the entrance to Tokyo Bay, less than a day's sail from Edo itself. Japanese guard boats teemed around the American flotilla, its lead boat bearing a standard that read in French: "Departez!" "Depart immediately and dare not anchor!" Every crew member on the American ships knew that, in the past, uninvited visitors to Japan had often been jailed, tortured, or decapitated. This time, however, the government was too weak to frighten the foreigners away, and the West had come to stay (figure 1.6).

In fact, Japan had been experiencing considerable internal turmoil, as regional clan leaders sought to secure their places in whatever structure would emerge from efforts to dislodge the Tokugawa clan. It was clear that the military dictatorship and the oppressive social hierarchy it tried to maintain were no longer functioning to keep peace within the country and manage affairs with external powers. The shogunate made some systematic attempts to modernize, sending embassies to the United States in 1860 and Europe in 1862, but it was too late. Without some kind of fresh internal structure and cohesion, there was a real possibility that Japan would become yet another colonized area. Choices were in the air.

FIGURE 1.6   *Japanese reception of the foreign vessels they called "black ships" after their color and the smoke bellowing from their engines.*   *(Courtesy of the Historiographical Institute, University of Tokyo. Shigetsu print. 1889.)*

MEIJI-PERIOD MODERNIZATION

The year 1868 is the date that officially marks a drastic change: with the support of those strong regional feudal lords who adroitly managed to consolidate their power, the long-powerless emperor was reinstated to the top of the political hierarchy, and a new era (the Meiji period, 1868–1912) had begun. The terms on which Meiji leaders chose to participate in the nineteenth-century globalizing political economy were decisive for the Japan we know today, an extremely powerful contemporary nation-state (figure 1.7).

Japanese leaders orchestrated an effective process of studying and adopting the tools for modernizing their country, similar in many respects to the way they studied and selected what they wanted from Korean and Chinese civilizations in the seventh to mid-ninth centuries (see chapter 2). Embassies were sent abroad to survey systematically aspects of European and American society, from school systems to imperial marriage celebrations. At a remarkably fast pace, a traditional economy based on agriculture was shifted to an economy based on industry. Edo, now Tokyo (literally the "eastern capital," to distinguish it from Kyoto, the imperial center), was finally recognized as the official capital, first among Japan's cities in a period of rapid urbanization. Understood to be the basis of the modernizing process, universal education was insti-

Pre-named period: to 645

Taika period: 645–710

Nara period: 710–784

Heian period: 794–1185

   Fujiwara period (Late Heian): 857–1160

Taira period: 1160–1185

Kamakura period: 1185–1333

Ashikaga (Muromachi) period: 1336–1573

Nobunaga: 1573–1582

Hideyoshi: 1582–1598

Tokugawa: 1598–

   established Tokugawa shogunate

Tokugawa (EDO) period: 1600–1868

Meiji period: 1868–1912

Taisho period: 1912–1926

Showa period: 1926–1989

Heisei period: 1989–

Dates in Japan are given according to the period. For example, our year 1989 would be given in Japan as Heisei 1.

FIGURE 1.7   *Timeline of Japanese history.*

tuted, with a federally managed school system that was and is an effective tool for communication with the population as a whole. By rapidly and successfully following the models established by European colonizing nations and the United States, the new government adroitly managed to keep Japan free of occupation.

In the design of the new classless educational system (based on that of the United States, the only such elementary school system in the West at the time), national cultural policy dictated that music would be included in the new primary school curriculum. The immediate model was public school instruction in Massachusetts, where music had recently been added to the comprehensive course of study. Still, did music have to be taught in the new Japanese schools? Many scholars have contended that it was just naturally included, as part of the package of elements adopted in the process of modernizing, but others have suggested more focused reasons.

The historian Ury Eppstein (1994) argues that the education sector followed the example of the military. Bands attached to foreign armies had appeared to Japanese observers to be a significant element in the military establishment. Japan's first brass band was formed by the powerful Satsuma clan in Meiji 2 (1869; the Japanese custom is to number their years beginning with each imperial reign, figure 1.7) with brass instruments imported from England; notably, the first version (now forgotten) of "Kimigayo" ("The Emperor's World"), Japan's national anthem, was arranged by this band and played before Emperor Meiji from 1871 to 1877 (Naito 1977: 7). Band music had also been observed by the surveyors sent by the Foreign Ministry to European courts to be an essential element of the "ceremonial style of governance" that the Meiji leaders cultivated as they sought to emulate and surpass the pomp and pageantry of European and North American governments (Fujitani 1996).

In the late nineteenth century, when the Japanese military was being built up as the ultimate extension of the Meiji government's power, the imperial army and navy took the most initiative in the appropriation of Western music: an official military band was founded in 1871 (Atkins 2001: 51). The military establishment valued music as a factor conducive to maintaining discipline and raising morale in the army and navy. Also, "military bands introduced to Japan not only standard band repertoire and instruments, but also orchestral instruments and piano, martial songs, Western singing style, and the public concert. In addition they encouraged composition" (May 1963: 43).

With the military setting the example, music was taken into the primary school curriculum. In education, it was deemed valuable for the spiritual and physical health and character formation of the pupils. While European music was the clear choice for the military bands, the selection of "apt music" for school children was not so clear. Shuji Izawa, the Japanese teacher who had experienced studying in Massachusetts, submitted a plan to the minister of education on 30 October 1879:

Let me take the liberty . . . of briefly stating the prevailing opinions as to the matter, which can be summed up essentially into three. The first says that, as music is the chief means which excites and stimulates our emotions, and as human passions are naturally expressed by musical tones, the same music might be universally used by all mankind, in spite of the differences of country or of race; and that European music has almost reached perfection by means of the contemplations and experience of the last thousand years, since the time of the Greek sage, Pythagoras, and it surpasses very greatly oriental music in perfection and beauty. It will, therefore, be far better to adopt European music in our schools than to undertake the awkward task of improving the imperfect oriental music.

The second says there are in every country and nation their own languages, customs, and usages, which being the natural outgrowth of the character of the people and the conditions of the land cannot be changed by human efforts. . . . We have never heard of any country in which the native music has been entirely supplanted by foreign music, and consequently to introduce European music into our country must, at least, be as useless an attempt as to adopt English as our language; therefore it will be a far wiser plan to take measures toward the cultivation and improvement of our own music.

The third says that the two former opinions are not entirely unreasonable, but they seem to run to the two opposite extremities of the matter, and hence, taking a middle course, the proper measure would be to secure the best from both European and oriental music. . . . If, fearing the difficulties, we do not presently undertake the work, when shall we see musical progress in Japan? (Cited in May 1963: 52–53)

One sentence in Izawa's report is particularly revealing as to one of the most devastating effects of the colonial system: "It will, therefore, be far better to adopt European music in our schools than to undertake the awkward task of improving the imperfect oriental music." The psychological effects of unequal relations are recognized to be as powerful as economic effects, and inculcation of the idea that the culture of the colonizer is superior was part of the system. Although foreign powers never colonized Japan on Japanese soil, the ideas were transmitted and believed. That is another significant reason for the choice of European music in the Japanese school curriculum.

At first, however, Izawa's third path was followed in the creation of songs for new textbooks. An American music educator, Luther Whiting Mason (1828–1886), whom Izawa had met in Massachusetts, was hired to work with Japanese specialists—notably, a distinguished player of *koto* (a zither), musicians of the imperial *gagaku* (court music) ensemble, and a poet. They assembled Western tunes for which Japanese texts were written, sophisticated adult music from *gagaku* or *koto* melodies, and also new songs with especially written texts. Japanese pieces were harmonized in the European tonal system.

While collaboration with Japanese musicians was attempted, it was problematic, and here is another significant reason for the initial dilemma about the choice of music for primary education: the situatedness of Japanese indigenous music within the Japanese social and cultural system. Each genre of music was clearly associated with some particular group of people and performance context; who made the music, for whom, and where really mattered, with implications of social status and morality. *Gagaku* (CD track 5) was the music of the imperial court and of Buddhist temple and Shinto shrine ceremonies; *koto* (CD track 6) was the instrument of elite and upper middle-class citizens; the *nō* drama (CD track 3) was the special purview of the elite and especially the *samurai* class; *syamisen*-accompanied songs (CD track 7) were particularly associated with the popular theater and adult entertainment world. None of them was appropriate for primary school education for the entire population of children. The dilemma was pragmatic as well as psychological.

European music was a solution to the dilemma: the meaning of European (i.e., foreign) music could be constructed as the same for all Japanese. Furthermore, its cultural status as translated in Japan was high, offering the possibility of putting Japanese into the cultural mainstream of those who wielded power over most of the world. For those who chose to make careers as performers of the European classical repertoire, it also offered prestige in the modernizing culture.

By 1883 the school songbooks contained mainly foreign pieces, and after 1890 the attempt to fuse "East and West" musically in primary school songs was abandoned entirely in favor of "the West." The texts of the Meiji school songs, however, were useful to the government, being "a combination of Confucian precepts of filial obedience and morality, and nationalistic indoctrination" (May 1959: 63). Sung in chorus—an activity natural from the widespread practice of communal singing of folk song—they could be quite stirring.

But another kind of music from the European tradition was exerting considerable influence at this crucial time: hymnody, specifically Protestant hymns, which many Japanese were now learning as missionaries again flooded into the newly opened nation. With their clear melodies, solid harmony, and predictable structure, they offered an attractive type of song through which schoolchildren could be enculturated into the European musical tradition. "Missionaries introduced the Christian hymn and hymnal, the Western concept of vocal tone, part singing, the Sol Fa system of sightreading, and the portable organ. They were largely, if not totally, responsible for the development of congregational singing, and their work contributed to the spread of general popular singing of Western melodies. Their hymns found their way into the school song books" (May 1959: 48). It is actually not a great leap from that sort of shared musical experience to the choruses of more than two hundred thousand singing the final movement of Beethoven's Symphony No. 9 (CD track 4) to celebrate the end of the old and beginning of the new year.

At first instruments were not easily or widely available. Luther Whiting Mason took to Japan a variety of them such as flutes, clarinets, cellos, and basses and about a dozen pianos. Thus orchestral instruments and pianos became part of the educational system. Furthermore, Mason gave instruction to the Japanese in the manufacture of the "American organ," the small reed organ used by the missionaries (May 1963: 59). These organs were found in schools that had difficulty in obtaining pianos and were used as piano substitutes by many families at least into the 1950s.

The piano, however, was the instrument of choice. Because every piano had to be imported at first, it was an instrument only the wealthy could afford. As a physical object also the piano offered certain challenges, as it was not easily incorporated into the traditional Japanese home. There were few areas of floor that were not covered with relatively fragile straw mats (*tatami*) and therefore few places the heavy instrument could be placed with proper support. The piano went into the wood-floored space for especially treasured items (*tokonoma*), thereby being accorded high status spatially, visually, and emblematically. For several reasons, then, its high cultural status in Europe was maintained in Japan. In the early twentieth century domestic production of European instruments by Japanese companies such as Yamaha burgeoned, making them relatively more easily available and affordable. The piano became the instrument that parents were most likely to have their children study for their personal development and upward social mobility.

As the years passed, music from Western cultures became increasingly embedded in Japanese life. Commercial enterprises put tonal music pervasively into urban soundscapes and greatly increased the enculturation of young musicians into the European musical system. Walking the streets, the earliest commercial brass bands advertised everything from makeup and toothbrushes to beer and tobacco, and department stores relied on them to attract customers.

The brass bands were superseded by department store youth troupes. Getting into the business of training young people who lacked both the social standing and the finances to go to the elite conservatories that had emerged for training in European classical music, Mitsukoshi Department Store, in the first two decades of the twentieth century, provided free training. The young musicians were then employed to perform in or around the stores to attract customers. Another commercial venture was the *bandoya* ("bands for hire"), independent businesses often run by former military bandsmen who trained musicians and then provided bands for movie theaters and galas as well as for advertising. Instrument makers, most particularly piano manufacturers such as Yamaha, also offered instruction as a means of aggressively selling their products. "Most of Japan's journeyman musicians—in the classical, jazz, and popular fields—were products of these organizations" (Atkins 2001: 53).

WORLD WAR I AND IMMEDIATELY FOLLOWING

Music and the military in Japan again came together in World War I (1914–18), but in a very different way. As an ally of England, Japan declared war against Germany and sent fifty thousand soldiers to Tsingtao in China. During that venture forty-six hundred German military were captured, among them the father of UCLA professor emeritus of history Hans Baerwald, who transmitted this account.

My father had arrived in Kobe (December 1912) as a German businessman. . . . As was the case with all able-bodied German males in Asia, the German Embassy sent him a draft notice—despite his never having handled any military implements—and ordered him to participate in the defense of the garrison in Tsingtao on the Shandung Peninsula, a German "concession" (small colony) shortly after the outbreak of the "first" World War in the late summer of 1914. His active career as a soldier was mercifully brief—September to November 1914—as Japan's military might was far superior. . . . He remained a prisoner of war of the Japanese government until the signing of the Versailles Peace Treaty in the spring of 1919, first in a temple in Matsuyama, Ehime Prefecture, and later in the camp known as "Bandō," the remnants of which are now located within Naruto City, Tokushima Prefecture [on Shikoku Island]. The latter has become famous for having been the site of the first performance of Beethoven's Ninth Symphony on Japanese soil, by the camp orchestra of which he was a member of the first violin section. A photograph of my father playing the violin with the POW orchestra is on display today in Bandō Museum in Naruto City (2002: 30–31).

Japanese musicians played in the orchestra as well:

> These POWs formed an orchestra with some local Japanese amateur musicians in Bandō, Shikoku Island, where the camp was set up. The favorite music played by this orchestra was Beethoven's Symphony no. 9, which later became one of the most popular pieces of classical music in Japan and now is played throughout the country toward the end of each year. (Inoue, Ozawa, Sakon, and Hosaka, 1996: 73)

∞

Ludwig van Beethoven (1770–1827) composed nine symphonies, all of which are important pieces in the European canon of today. The Ninth was extraordinary at the time, however, as it was the first instance of a symphony that called for a chorus as well as full orchestra. That chorus occurs in the fourth (last) movement. With the exception of a few lines by Beethoven himself, the sung text is drawn from a poem, the "Ode to Joy" ("An die Freude," first published in 1785) by the great German poet Friedrich Schiller (1759–1805). As composers commonly do, Beethoven selected portions to assemble a text for his own purpose: suggesting a path to Utopia, a goal-directed progression from joy, through brotherhood, then to prayer, and finally to a combination of all three.

∞

ACTIVITY 1.1 *With this history of the first performance in mind, listen first to the very short portion of the finale that is recorded on CD track 4. Listen and sing along with the melody until you have learned it aurally:*

Deine Zauber binden wieder,	Thy magic binds up again
Was die Mode streng geteilt;	What custom sternly divided;
Alle Menschen werden Bruder,	All men become brothers,
Wo dein sanfter Flugel weilt.	Here thy gentle wing prevails.

Then find a full recording of the whole movement. The chorale theme is introduced only gradually, but if you have learned it you will hear its first occurrence, then second. Beethoven has com-

> posed a kind of conversation among the orchestra, sections of the orchestra (listen for the string basses), a baritone soloist, and finally, the chorus. Just before the chorus enters, the baritone soloist asserts himself, with text composed by Beethoven. "Joy" is then proclaimed by the baritone as the link to Schiller's text, with the chorus chiming in.
>
> As you listen, think about the meaning of this piece in Japan.
>
> "For many Japanese the Ninth Symphony is important to listen to at year end; it does not mean the Christmas season. The Ninth Symphony shows the power of salvation and peace so that it matches the Japanese wish to close a year peacefully, believing that "all is well that ends well" (Kazuko Nakajima, personal communication, 2000).

"By virtue of being on the "right side" in World War I, Asia's pre-eminent power was thus included [albeit as an unequal partner, as the terms of the Versailles treaty proved] in the community of victor nations and [Japan] achieved an unprecedented degree of political, economic, military, and cultural integration with that international community she had sought to join." (Atkins 2001: 95)

The years between the two world wars (during the Taisho period, 1912–26, and beginning of the Showa period, 1926–89, each era named by a new emperor) found Japan situated to make further choices. There was considerable disagreement and debate among political and intellectual leaders, those favoring cosmopolitan choices (that is, participation in the global culture and economy), and those militantly asserting cultural traditionalism. But even as debate at the top heated up, an emerging urban middle class made lifestyle and consumption choices similar to those made by their counterparts in "the West."

By the middle of the Taisho period "dance fever" had struck, and social dances for couples such as the two-step and fox trot had become necessary skills for the upscale "modernite" (Atkins 2001: 54). The American correspondent Grace Seton reported in *Metronome* (July 1923):

The Japanese are jazzing by day and by night. The "foreign craze" trips merrily on its way through the sacred traditions of Nipponese etiquette and of the home. . . . Girls and young married women man-

age the intricate steps of the jazz in tabi and zori [traditional foot-
ware] with surprising ease. . . .

Foreign dancing undoubtedly has come to stay. It is much in evidence in Tokio [sic] and has spread into Yokohama, Osaka and Kobe,
although not to any extent outside of the big cities. The majority of
dancers are foreign-trained students, who got the spirit of the dance by
contact with Western life. What will be the effect upon national life is a
problem occupying many thinking Japanese. In the main they approve
of it—with reservations. That is, they approve of the social principle it
involves, of bringing young people together in a more informal way.

The dance craze offered a livelihood for hundreds of aspiring young
musicians who found employment in hotel ballrooms or salon orchestras aboard ocean liners. Trained initially in the rudiments of the music in the primary schools, and also in conservatories or the department
store troupes and *bandoya*, many learned as well from Filipino artists
who had had opportunity to acquire popular music styles from their
American occupiers. Fiipino musicians dominated the bands on ocean
liners and in the entertainment venues in Japanese cities such as Kobe
that catered to foreigners. The saxophonist and composer Ryoichi
Hattori (1907–93) credited the Filipino influence: "Their musical sense
and performance technique were amazing. It could be said that they were
the 'parents' who raised Japanese jazzmen" (cited in Atkins 2001: 59).

American musicians did not visit Japan in sufficient numbers before
the late 1920s to constitute a vital source for aspiring Japanese jazz musicians, but recordings imported from America did. Supported by foreign capital, a number of companies in Japan—most prominently Poly-
dor, Nippon Columbia, and Nippon Victor—marketed imported
records of popular and classical music from America and Europe.

Thus, music of "the West" became a part of Japanese culture by several means and for multiple reasons. From primary school education
Japanese students were enculturated with the basic elements—the tonal
system, with its chordal harmony and metrically felt rhythm. Increasingly, the entire population absorbed them through what they heard in
the urban soundscapes and from the electronic media. Participation in
the making of European classical music and popular musics from North
and South America simply exploded from practically nonexistent in the
1880s to a viable mode for earning a living in the global market for music in the 1920s, a span of only forty short years. Participation in traditional musical genres continued, of course, but prestige and economic
opportunities offered in the sphere of European and then American music pulled the populace farther and farther away from indigenous styles.

CHAPTER 2

International Interface: Looking Eastward

∞

TRADITION IN A TIME OF CHANGE

In the symbolic persona of the emperor and the rites attendant thereto, one can clearly see Japan's long tradition of interface with other cultures. On 9 March 1894 the celebration was held of the twenty-fifth wedding anniversary of Emperor Meiji. Not a moment marked traditionally in Japan, a committee had been formed to study similar celebrations of European monarchies. An account of the resulting events provides entree to the manner in which history and modernization were self-consciously brought together in the Meiji era.

> The core ceremonies [of the resulting event on 9 March] began within the sacred and invisible confines of the Palace Sanctuary, continued into the public rooms of the palace where Japanese and foreign dignitaries observed them, and culminated with an imperial military review at the Aoyama Military Parade Field [to which the] emperor and empress rode together out of the palace in a state ceremonial carriage.
>
> The celebration continued into the night at the palace with a banquet and performance of bugaku, the ancient court music and dancing [figure 2.1]. Many of the guests, echoing the matrimonial theme, came as couples. . . . The emperor and empress entered both the banquet hall and the Throne Room for the bugaku arm in arm, further demonstrating their modern and civilized conjugal relationship. . . . For the bugaku performance the emperor and empress sat side by side on their thrones upon a dais that had been specially erected for the occasion. (Fujitani 1996: 113–15)

FIGURE 2.1 Bugaku *dance: "Taisōtoku," a dance of old men.* *(Photo by permission of the* Gagaku *Music Society of Tenri University.)*

INTERFACE IN THE FIRST MILLENNIUM

Understanding the inclusion of a performance of *bugaku* in that day of ceremonies takes us back to the early centuries of the first millennium, when a selection of instruments, compositions (including *bugaku* dance pieces), and ensemble practices were introduced to Japan from China, Korea, and other parts of Asia through processes similar to those just related for the introduction of European and American music. All that imported instrumentarium and music is now called *gagaku* (literally, "proper" music, but more usually translated as "imperial court music").

Contact between Japanese and Koreans (and peoples in the regions just to the north of the Korean peninsula) began very early and has been continuous; they are related physically and linguistically. Cultural exchange has occurred in both directions. The first recorded visit of musicians to Japan was by eighty performers from Korea's Silla kingdom in 453. Archaeological records show that through movement of peoples, elements of Korean lifestyles such as jewelry and clothing, agricultural techniques, and types of pottery were absorbed into the culture of Japan in the fifth and sixth centuries. Conversely, the rulers of the Yamato culture, the first political entity to begin to control large areas within Japan, had a foothold in southern Korea in the fourth through sixth centuries.

Because Korean culture was heavily involved with that of China, Korea was also a conduit through which elements of continental civilization were introduced to Japan. Buddhism is a good example: "It probably drifted into the islands over a period of time, but its official introduction is dated in 552 (though probably more accurately in 538) when the Korean state of Paekche presented an image and scriptures to the Yamato court" (Fairbank, Reischauer, and Craig 1973: 327–35). Buddhism became a vehicle for the transfer of much Chinese culture to Japan, just as Christianity served as a vehicle for the transfer of European civilization to Japan a millennium later.

Japanese contact with China had been occurring for some time. Direct contact by envoys with China occurred at least as early as the year 57 and travelers from Japan had reached the Chinese court as early as the third century. For the most part however, the contact was a slow, unpurposeful process until the introduction of Buddhism. At that point, the Japanese began to take steps to transplant elements of the continental culture (just as they did centuries later with Western culture). The process escalated in the seventh century, as the powerful and sophisticated Chinese Tang court (618–907) became one of the most cosmopolitan cultural centers ever known in history. Embassies were sent in 607, 608, and 614 by Japan's ruler, Shotoku, and others followed later.

The importance of these embassies to the Japanese can be judged from their size and the extreme perils they braved. By the eighth century it was customary to build four new ships for each mission, and some five hundred to six hundred men were sent. Disasters were frequent because the Japanese attempted to sail directly to China across five hundred miles of open sea, without benefit of compass or much knowledge of the seasonal winds. "The significance of the missions lay, not in their diplomatic achievements or incidental trade, but in what the Japanese participants learned in China. Students of all sorts accompanied the missions—Buddhist monks, scholars of Chinese history and literature, painters, musicians, and others. Studying during the year the mission was in China or possibly for several years until the next mission brought them home, these men acquired knowledge and skills that were highly regarded at the Japanese court and contributed greatly to the cultural transformation of the country" (Fairbank, Reischauer, and Craig 1973: 336). Although the Japanese language is unrelated to the

Chinese language, the Chinese writing system was adopted, and along with it a love of calligraphy and of poetry. Chinese ideas, tastes, and other systems were adopted as well: Confucian virtues of loyalty and duty; centralized government with a new capital (Nara) designed on the model of the Tang capital of Chang-an (now Xian), holding the ruler supreme but supported by a meritocracy, and the high status of scholarship on which it depended; architectural techniques and painting styles; court rituals and ceremonials; and most pertinently here, musical instruments and repertoire performed on them.

As with other aspects of Tang court life in China, the musical culture was cosmopolitan and international. In addition to music for a number of formal ceremonies and rituals, courtiers and guests were entertained by musicians from numerous places—regions of East Asia beyond their borders, Central Asia, and India among them. A primary reason was the tremendous flow of peoples and goods along what we call now the "Silk Road" that began in the Mediterranean region and ended in Chang-an. Instruments now taken for granted by many people as being indigenously Chinese were being newly imported there—not the instruments as exotic objects traded along with other artifacts, but as living culture, with foreign musicians playing them. Thus it was a variety of instruments and styles of music that musicians in the Japanese embassies encountered, studied, and transported back home. Foreign musicians immigrated to Japan as well.

Origins of pieces that were imported are remembered today. Pieces known to have been Chinese or from areas of Asia to the south and west of China (for example, Southeast Asia and India) are referred to as the *tōgaku* (music of the left) repertoire. Pieces known to have come from parts of Asia to the north (ie, Korea and the area north of it now known as Manchuria) are called the *komagaku* (music of the right) repertoire.

Historic instruments are known today because of an incredible storehouse, the Imperial Shosoin, on the grounds of the Todaiji Buddhist temple in Nara. On the twenty-first day of the sixth month of the year 756, the large building was dedicated by the Empress Dowager Komyo in honor of the forty-ninth day (the seven-times-seventh day) from the death of the Emperor Shomu. Into the storehouse were placed most of the household materials of the imperial home including musical instruments, along with a catalog. The largest additions to the storehouse were made in 950, when another warehouse was destroyed (Malm 1983: 5). Fires have always been an extreme danger in Japan, where many buildings are wood, as is the Shosoin, and it is simply amazing that the building has survived. Its precious contents, designated as National Treasures, have for some time been housed in a concrete building nearby for safekeeping. Available for viewing just once a year by designated officials, the collection remains a historical source of inestimable value that even highly respected individuals unfortunately have little chance to see.

The high point of Chinese cultural influence was reached in the beginning of the Heian period (794–1185) in Japan, when the capital was in Kyoto. In the course of the ninth century there was a slow but major shift to a long period of indigenization of the imported culture and to domestic creativity. From the Shosoin collection it is clear that the variety of instruments imported in the Nara (710–84) and Heian (794–1185) periods is far greater than that played by musicians who perform *gagaku* music today. The next section introduces instruments that have remained in use, with some comment on their musical roles in *gagaku* as it is performed at present.

THE *GAGAKU* ENSEMBLE AS WE HEAR IT

A full range of instrument types can be found in the *gagaku* ensemble, the largest ensemble in all of Japanese traditional music. I present them here in terms of the international (Sachs-Hornbostel) classification system. The *gagaku* instruments fall into the four categories of aerophones, chordophones, membranophones, and idiophones. Due to the distinct timbres of the instruments, except for the chordophones, one can distinctly hear each instrument's part in the music; it is a heterogeneous sound ideal, resulting in a sort of stylistic transparency. As you read the subsections on aerophones and chordophones that follow, use CD

track 8 to listen for each instrument.

CD track 8 is a brief prelude (*netori*) whose function is to introduce the melodic mode of a named piece that will follow in performance. There are six modes used in *tōgaku*, each with a different fundamental pitch (see Wade 2004 for a discussion of melodic mode). CD track 8 introduces a mode (*chō*) called *banshiki*, the ancient Japanese name for the pitch B, the tonal center of this mode. In the cosmology of *gagaku* that was transmitted from China, *banshiki* is associated with the element water, the virtue of knowledge, and the direction north. Winter is its seasonal association. *Banshiki* is also identified with the color black and symbolizes the darkness and fecundity of the womb. Linked to rituals of the imperial household, this mode exclusively is used for funeral ceremonies of the imperial family. For the funeral procession of Emperor Meiji, the composition "Manjūraku" ("Music of Ten Thousand Autumns") in *banshiki* mode was played continuously from the palace in downtown Tokyo to a ceremonial place near the Meiji Shrine, a distance of some four miles. "Senshūraku" ("Music of a Thousand Autumns"), also in *banshiki*, was played as the remains were lowered into the tomb. The *netori* in CD track 8 introduces you to the feeling and the pitches of *banshiki* mode, but the musical character of the prelude also permits you to hear the instruments clearly.

Aerophones.   Three different types of wind instrument are used in the ensemble: flute, double reed, and mouth organ. Flutes (generically, *fue*) occur in three sizes (see figure 2.2 for two of them). The *ryūteki* is played for the *tōgaku* repertoire that originated in south, and west of, China. The *komabue* is played for *komagaku* pieces from Korea and Manchuria. Both flutes are made of bamboo but are lacquered inside to prevent moisture from accumulating and to make the sound clearer than the usual soft sound of a bamboo flute. The outside is wrapped with cherry tree bark for aesthetic purposes. The *gagaku flutes* are transverse flutes, held horizontally.

The *hichiriki* is a double-reed aerophone held vertically; like the flute, it is made of bamboo with a hardened interior (figure 2.3). The resonant timbre and volume of sound produced on such a small instrument is remarkable. Multiple *hichiriki* heard together in a type of prelude called *chōshi* produce an eerie but wonderful sound to my ears (CD track 9); this longer type of instrumental prelude is played as a prelude or entrance music for dance performances, and also in Buddhist ceremonies for the anniversary of a death.

Frequently called a "mouth organ" because of both its construction and its sound, the *shō* consists of seventeen bamboo pipes resting in a wind chamber (figure 2.4). A mouthpiece extends out from the chamber. Each of fifteen of the pipes is fitted with a small metal reed inside that vibrates with the player's breath when the small hole in the side of the pipe is stopped. As you can see in figure 2.5, the *shō* is not usually played for pieces in the *komagaku* repertoire; the resulting ensemble sound is sparse compared to the sound of the *tōgaku* ensemble, which does include the *shō* (CD track 5 *komagaku* compared to CD track 8).

The flutes, double reed, and mouth organ all have melodic roles in *gagaku* music. Flutes and the double reed play the melody of compositions heterophonically (that is, one melody in slightly different versions simultaneously). Important to the flute parts in the music are the dis-

FIGURE 2.2 Fue *(flutes) for* gagaku. *Top:* Komabue, *bottom:* ryūteki. *Formerly, the bamboo tube was carefully split into several sections, which were reversed and fitted together again so that the hard smooth outer surface became the inside of the tube. These sections once carefully fitted together were tightly wrapped with bark all around except at the holes. Now, the natural tube is lacquered inside for the same effect.* *(Photo by Shinji Aoki.)*

FIGURE 2.3 Hichiriki *(double-reed). It has the outer appearance of a short inverted cone, thick where the reed is held, then narrow from the first fingerhole to the end. The inner bore, however, is cylindrical.* *(Photo by Shinji Aoki.)*

FIGURE 2.4 Shō *(mouth organ). Two pipes do not sound, being there for the symmetrical shape of a bird's wings.* *(Photo by Shinji Aoki.)*

tinctive melodic ornaments and the production of pitches by the closing of only half a fingerhole. Different timbres are produced in the *hichiriki* part, and microtonal ornaments embellishing pitch connections are important.

In the Heian period, the *shō* parts were much more melodic than they are now. In named *gagaku* pieces (as opposed to preludes) as we hear them now, the *shō* usually sounds clusters of tones rather than successive pitches. Since the instrument can be sounded either by inhalation or exhalation, the player can maintain a continuous stream of sound, thickening the texture considerably and "gluing together" the diverse sounds produced on the other instruments. However, the *shō* is still given a subtle, albeit abstracted melodic role. If you listen closely to CD

Kangen (instrumental)		*Bugaku* (dance)	
<u>*Tōgaku*</u>	<u>*Komagaku*</u>	<u>*Tōgaku*</u>	<u>*Komagaku*</u>
(China, Southeast Asia, India)	(Korea, Manchuria)		
Ryūteki	*Komabue*	*Ryūteki*	*Komabue*
Hichiriki	*Hichiriki*	*Hichiriki*	*Hichiriki*
Shō		*Shō*	
Sō no koto			
Biwa			
Kakko	*San no tsuzumi*	*Kakko*	*San no tsuzumi*
Shōko	*Shōko*	*Shōko*	*Shōko*
Taiko	*Taiko*	*Taiko*	*Taiko*
			(a large form, *ō-daiko*)

FIGURE 2.5   *Instrumentarium of gagaku ensembles.*

track 10, you can hear those individual pitches as the player shifts from one cluster to another in this way: the fundamental pitch of the first cluster is the last released, and the fundamental of the next is sounded first in the process of shifting.

Chordophones.   The two stringed instruments are the *biwa* and the *sō no koto*. While their sounds are similar, they are different types of instruments morphologically: lute and zither, respectively.

The *biwa* is a large, heavy, ovoid-shaped wooden lute with a very short neck (figure 2.6). Because it is plucked with a wooden plectrum, a broad strip of leather covers the striking area to protect the wood of the body. On the short, narrow neck are four small, raised, fixed frets and the uppermost bridge; the player puts his fingers not directly on the frets but just behind them.

The *sō no koto* (or *koto*, as the court musicians refer to it) is a zither just over six feet long, made from soft pawlonia wood (figure 2.7). Each of its thirteen strings is tuned by positioning a small bridge under it;

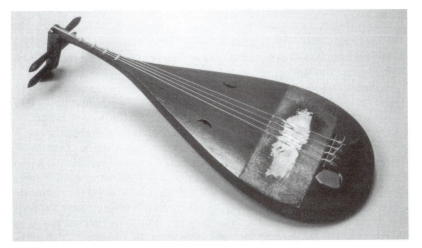

FIGURE 2.6 Gaku biwa. *Each of the four strings is of different thickness (the lower pitched, the thicker), made of strands of silk thread wound together. The pegs holding the strings are perpendicular to the neck, placing the lute's origin in the Middle East, from where players brought it across Asia to China (where it is known as the* pipa). *Unlike the lutes of the Middle East and Europe now, the* biwa *has a flat back and shallow resonating chamber. In this photo the plectrum is seen emerging from a leather pouch at the rounded end.* (Photo by Shinji Aoki.)

FIGURE 2.7 Sō no koto. *The koto is about six feet long and ten inches wide, with a slightly convex curve, carved from half a tree trunk. The grain of the wood is important both for visual aesthetics and to indicate the quality of sound. The bottom is closed in with a flat slab of wood, with sound holes at either end. Thirteen strings of uniform thickness are attached at the right playing end and stretched over the length of the instrument (hence its classification as a zither). At the right end, each string is pushed up from inside the sounding chamber through a small hole just beyond the fixed bridge, pulled to the far end, where it is pushed down through a small hole just beyond the lower fixed bridge into the sounding chamber, then out through the sound hole, to be pulled up over the end of the instrument, knotted to itself close to that bridge and decorously coiled there. The silk strings break easily from being struck/plucked only at the right end. To fix a broken string, the extra length is uncoiled and pulled up. Strings on modern kotos are made of synthetic materials, but are attached in the same way (see figure 3.4).* (Photo by Shinji Aoki.)

the highest pitch is closest to the player. The bridges can be moved easily to change the tuning.

Rather than playing melody along with the aerophones as one might expect on a lute or zither, the *biwa* and *sō no koto* parts just underline the melody by sounding strategic pitches at rhythmically important points. In effect, they function as a bridge between the melodic parts and the percussion instruments. The *koto* part is in a sparse, preserved state, consisting of octave patterns and single tones played at the same moments as the *biwa* is played. For that reason and others, hearing these chordophones requires close listening. With silk strings, their sounds are relatively soft and die away quickly. Furthermore, their timbres blend together. Watching the *biwa* players, it is clear that preparation for striking the strings and then relaxing with the plectrum after playing is almost as important as what is played—a downward stroking across the strings leading to a single bold stroke on the string that sounds the melodic pitch. The technique is ceremonial, even highly ritualized.

The sparse, formulaic parts of the strings are greatly changed from Heian times, owing mostly to a socio-musical reason: during the Heian period, these two instruments were the purview of members of the nobility rather than the employed court musicians. Consensus opinion among scholars recently is that the old, more melodic performance practice—even possibly improvisation—on the stringed instruments was lost when nobles lost interest in playing them. For this reason, generations of professional court and Buddhist temple musicians are to be credited for having preserved the *gagaku* performance tradition as we are able to know it now.

Membranophones and an Idiophone. Two percussion instruments are a mainstay in every full ensemble—the *taiko* and the *shōko*. The *taiko* is the membranophone of the frame drum type (figure 2.8). Its two heads of oxhide are tacked onto the wooden frame—a method of attachment used widely in East Asia. The rounded ends of the two laquered wooden drumsticks are padded with leather. The sound of the *taiko* is strong, dark, and resonant.

In contrast, a high, bright sound is produced by the *shōko*, a shallow bronze idiophone of the gong type (figure 2.9). It is played with two long sticks with bare wooden ends that are loosely held together by a silken cord.

The drum and gong are both suspended high on standing wooden frames such that the players (seated on the floor as all the musicians

FIGURE 2.8 *The* gagaku taiko *is a frame drum in that the width of the frame (ca. 3.6 inches) is smaller than the diameter of the heads (ca. 20 inches). Decorated in bright colors, the heads picture frolicking lions or some mythological emblem such as the dragon.*   (Photo by Shinji Aoki.)

FIGURE 2.9 Shōko. *The bronze of the gong is just under one inch in width; the diameter is five inches. It hangs suspended by silk cords from a lacquered wooden frame that puts the instrument at a height just below the player's eye level. When not in use, the sticks are suspended from the top middle of the frame.*   (Photo by Shinji Aoki.)

FIGURE 2.10   Kakko. *Each head, larger (10 inches diameter) than the diameter of the body (6$\frac{1}{2}$ inches) is mounted onto a circular frame. The heads are held tight to the drum body by lashing of silk or hemp from frame to frame. That lashing can be tightened by a cord, as shown. When not in use, the sticks rest on the crossbar of the stand.   (Photo by Shinji Aoki.)*

are) must reach up to play them. Like the playing of the *biwa*, the raising of the arms to strike and the return to a resting position take on the appearance of ritual movement. Of course, one must be seated in just the right place to see the drama, because the players are behind the instruments. The *shōko* player strikes the inside of his gong that faces away from the audience, and the drummer likewise hits the skin that is hidden.

The ensembles for *tōgaku* and *komagaku* repertoires are also distinguished from each other by one percussion instrument. In CD track 8, the *banshiki* mode *netori*, you can hear a membranophone used only for performance of *tōgaku* repertoire—the *kakko* (figure 2.10). The *kakko* is a small barrel-shaped wooden drum that is placed on a low wooden stand. It has two deerhide heads, each played with a slender, slightly knobbed drumstick that is loosely held between thumb and index finger. Performances of *komagaku* pieces call for the *san no tsuzumi* (figure 2.11, CD track 5). Anyone familiar with Korean music will recognize the similarity to the distinctive shape of the *chang-gu* (see Wade 2004). The body of the *san no tsuzumi* is hourglass shaped. Imported to China from farther west in Asia, this type of drum was popular in the

FIGURE 2.11   San no tsuzumi. *The hourglass shape (otherwise described as "waisted" or "double-cup" shape) is narrow in the middle and open to both sides. The heads (12 inches diameter) are considerably larger than the openings of the body. As on the* kakko, *the heads are held together by lashing between the two of them; the tension is regulated by the center cord.   (Photo by Shinji Aoki.)*

Tang court, and was played in the ensemble there for Korean music. In present-day *gagaku* it is played with only one stick, striking only one side.

ACTIVITY 2.1   *To review the instruments, listen again to the* netori *on CD track 8, played by a* tōgaku *ensemble. Check each off in figure 2.5 as you identify it by sound. Then note which two* tōgaku *instruments do not play in* netori.

Listen as well, however, for these additional characteristics of netori.

1. In every performance of *netori* the instruments will enter and drop out in ritualized order. Identify that order.

2. To understand why this prelude is called *netori* (literally, "pulling sound"), listen for the non-pulsed rhythmic feel. The best way to get it is to try (fruitlessly) to find a steady beat. The phys-

icality of this music making is attuned more to the flexible pacing of breathing than to the regular pulsation of heartbeats. This "breathing rhythm" is an important aesthetic element in a good deal of Japanese traditional music. The very slow speed of *netori* provides a particularly clear illustration of it.

Finally, write a summary of everything you have learned about netori.

PERCUSSION PARTS IN *GAGAKU* MUSIC

As it survives today, *gagaku* music features instrumental parts that are more limited technically than the instruments themselves permit. Stylistic limitations have been rigidly preserved in the training system for the younger musicians, with great care taken in such things as exactness of breathing and phrasing and in the interpretation of the music. I shall turn to the percussion parts to demonstrate how, with very few techniques, "maximum musical effect has been achieved from a minimum of means," to quote the music scholar William Malm. For the explanation below, I draw on a source provided by Eta Harich-Schneider, who worked with Imperial Household musicians for a number of years and published a translation (1954) of three brush-written partbooks for the percussion instruments that are housed in the library of the Imperial Music Department. They had been compiled by musicians in the Imperial Household ensemble in the ninth year of Meiji (1876), then revised and confirmed in the twentieth year of Meiji (1887).

Strokes and Stroke Sequences. *Kakko* players use only three types of stroke (or technique). In the notation, each type is indicated by a *kanji* character (ideogram adopted from Chinese writing). The strokes are as follows.

Sei (正) A single stroke with the right stick, which is allowed to bounce lightly against the head. (The bouncing is difficult to hear on recordings.)

Katarai (來, pronounced *"rai"*) A slow accelerating roll played with the left stick alone. Usually followed by a *sei* stroke. If the musical part calls for more than one *katarai* in succession, right and left hand alternate, with the last turn taken by the left hand and followed by an accented *sei*.

Mororai (**來 來**, left and right "*rai*") A slow roll executed by the alternation of both sticks. While it might be heard to accelerate slightly right at the beginning, it is mostly steady.

Long ago, sequences of these strokes were established, to be played in various musical circumstances. *Netori* in *banshiki* mode will always have the sequence of *kakko* strokes shown in figure 2.12, for instance.

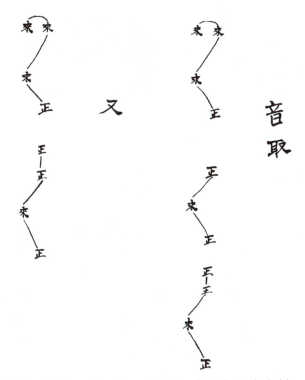

FIGURE 2.12 Kakko *pattern in* netori. *On the right is the* kakko *pattern for* netori *in* hyōjō *mode (Wade 2004, CD track 26); on the left is the pattern for* banshiki *mode (this text, CD track 8).*

ACTIVITY 2.2 *To identify the sequence of* kakko *strokes in* banshiki *mode, listen to CD track 8 with this guide. Do not expect to hear a clear separation between the end of* katarai *and the following* sei. *Listen several times and "drum" along with the recording.*

0:29 *mororai* (steady roll)

0:34 *katarai* (accelerating roll)

0:37 *sei* (sharp stroke)

0:38 *sei* (sharp stroke)

0:41 *katarai* (accelerating roll)

0:47 *sei* (sharp stroke)

Once you are comfortable with the stroke sequence, follow the notation of it in figure 2.12. Practice drawing the characters for these three strokes. Then find them in the notations in figure 2.13.

The *taiko* and *shōko* join the *kakko* in named compositions such as "Etenraku" (CD track 10) that follow the prelude. The strokes on these two instruments are even more limited. The player of the *shōko* must always hit the center of the gong where the tone will always be high and relatively ringing; not particularly clear, however, because after striking the center on the inside, in one continuous motion the stick is moved down to the lower rim, thus damping the sound. He (traditionally, all professional *gagaku* musicians have been male) plays in only two ways: a single stroke, spoken as "chin" (金), is played with either the left or the right stick, and a fast double stroke (left-right) is "chi-chin" (金 金). The drummer at the *taiko* sits slightly turned to the left, taking care that the left hand strikes somewhat left of the center of the drumface, whereas the right-hand stroke must hit directly into the center. The quiet left-hand stroke is considered a "female stroke," while the strong right-hand stroke is a "male stroke." The most common sequence is a "both-hands stroke" popularly referred to as *zun-dō*, with one beat separating *zun* and *dō* (Harich-Schneider 1954: 5). The two strokes are notated with a small and a large dot, which you can see in the notations in figure 2.13.

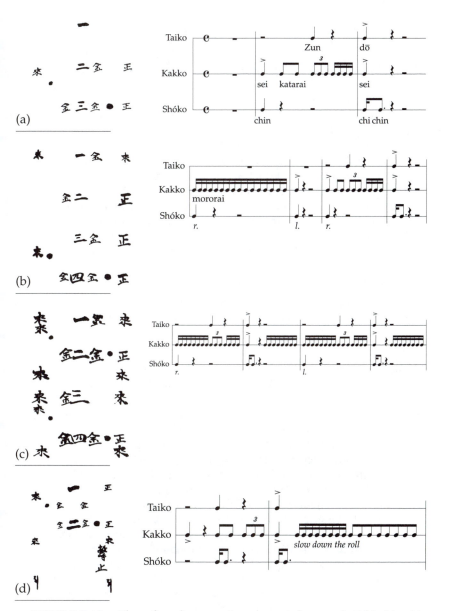

FIGURE 2.13 *Chart of* gagaku *percussion patterns in* haya yo hyōshi: *(a)* uchi-hajime *(beginning beats), opening pattern for named composition in* haya yo hyōshi; *(b) regular pattern; (c)* kuwaheru *(accumulation) pattern; (d)* uchidome, *ending pattern.*

Coordinated Percussion Patterns. Thus far you have learned about strokes and stroke sequences played on the percussion instruments. In named compositions you also meet coordinated percussion patterns where the three instruments interact in fixed ways. This is the earliest documented instance of a musical practice that occurs in a number of traditional Japanese musical genres.

The coordinated percussion patterns sound out a *hyōshi*, a metric structure. "Etenraku" (CD track 10) is in *haya yo hyōshi*: a structure that is four (*yo*) measures long, each measure consisting of four beats (*haya*) in medium speed. An entire coordinated pattern in *haya yo hyōshi*, then, takes sixteen counts to complete (four measures of four beats each).

There are several metric structures in *gagaku* music. Most of them are duple and symmetrical in structure (i.e., very Chinese), as shown here:

Medium speed:

haya yo hyōshi	4 (*yo*) measures of 4 beats (*haya*) each
haya ya hyōshi	8 (*ya*) measures of 4 beats (*haya*) each

Slow speed:

nobe yo hyōshi	4 (*yo*) measures of 8 beats (*nobe*) each
nobe ya hyōshi	8 (*ya*) measures of 8 beats (*nobe*) each

Not all *hyōshi* are duple, however. *Yatara byōshi* has an uneven structure, alternating measures of two and three beats.

A single piece will call for several coordinated percussion patterns. There is a coordinated pattern for beginning a composition (*uchihajime*, or "beginning the beating") that occurs just once but gives all the ensemble players an opportunity to settle into regular beats (figure 2.13a). Then there is a "regular pattern" that, of all the patterns, most clearly articulates the metric structure (*hyōshi*) of the particular piece (figure 2.13b); a regular pattern will be repeated several times, accelerating gradually. In most pieces there comes a moment when the number of *taiko* strokes doubles or triples and the *kakko* and *shōko* parts are adjusted accordingly; they are playing the *kuwaheru* pattern ("accumulation") (figure 2.13c). Slowing to end, in some pieces there is a final stroke sequence (*uchidome*) ending with *kakko* only (figure 2.13d).

An aesthetic shape is created from beginning to end of the piece by means of the coordinated percussion patterns: beginning slowly with a sense of beats but not quite regular, settling down to regular beats and gradually accelerating, gathering to a sort of climactic density, then ending with thinning texture and deceleration. That aesthetic shape is termed *jo-ha-kyū*. On a grander scale, multi-movement suites follow the same aesthetic structure, begun with the rhythmically flexible and slow prelude-type movements (*netori* and *chōshi*, generically termed *jo*), followed by a medium-speed named movement with a metric structure (*ha*), and a fast, metered movement with the same name (*kyū*).

Once the "regular pattern" begins, the percussion instruments articulate the metric structure of a named piece, working in coordination through the fixed patterns. From *hyōshi* to *hyōshi* the metric function of each instrument within a pattern is consistent: the *kakko* keeps the rhythm moving; the *shōko* articulates especially the first count of measures; and the *taiko* signals the larger framework of the whole structure. Even if you cannot read staff notation, you can see this visually in figure 2.13b.

In the Japanese notation of figure 2.13b, the "regular pattern" of *hayayohyōshi* notation, the measures are shown with Chinese/Japanese numbers (1 — 2 二 3 三 4 四) displayed vertically, as those languages are written. Individual beats within measures are not notated because performers learn aurally where to place their strokes. Just to the left and right of the numbers the *shōko* strokes are shown, with the Chinese character for "metal" (金): the position at left or right indicates which hand should play the stroke spoken as "*chin*"; a quick "*chi-chin*" is indicated by showing that character on both sides of the measure number. You can use the *shōko* strokes to count: "*chin*" 2 3 4 "*chin*" 2 3 4 "*chin*" 2 3 4 "*chi-chin*" 2 3 4. That *shōko* stroke sequence repeats as long as the "regular pattern" is being played. When the percussion density increases in the *kuwaheru* pattern (figure 2.13c), "*chi-chin*" is played in the second measure as well.

Just to the left and right of the *shōko* strokes, the *taiko* strokes are notated: a small dot for *zun* and a large dot for *dō*. In the "regular" pattern shown in figure 2.13b, *zun* occurs on beat 3 of the third measure, and *dō* is heard strongly on the first beat of the fourth measure. The *zun-dō* sequence is played twice as frequently in the *kuwaheru* pattern.

On the far left and right, the *kakko* strokes are notated. In the "regular" pattern in figure 2.13b, the *mororai* even roll creates motion through all four beats of the first measure, ending with *sei* on the first count of measure 2. The *katarai* accelerating roll creates motion through all four beats of measure 3, ending with *sei* on the first count of measure 4. The *kakkō* becomes even more active in the *kuwaheru* pattern.

The strongest beat in the coordinated pattern is clearly the first count of measure 4, where all three instruments coincide.

ACTIVITY 2.3 *With friends, establish a regular beat and "drum" the patterns in figures 2.13b, c, and d to embody the three metric coordinated patterns. The "*kakko *player" alone ends the shorter two-measure* uchidome *pattern.*

Then listen to CD track 10 from beginning to end, tracking the succession of the patterns.

- At 0.17 catch the *taiko dō* stroke of the short *uchihajime* pattern (figure 2.13a).

- From that point, try to find the beat. Patience is required, owing to the performance practice of "breathing rhythm" rather than pulsation. Gradually a beat will become clearer.

- The next task is to identify the measures. Listen for the *taiko dō* strokes and make a timing chart of them through the whole selection. Hint: the first *dō* in the regular pattern is at 0:49; then they occur at 1:24, 1:56, and so forth. At the *dō* stroke start counting the beats of the fourth measure: 4-2-3-4 1-2-3-4 2-2-3-4 3-2-3-4 4-2-3-4 and so forth. One further hint: the last *dō* in the regular pattern occurs at 3:22; (I made two splices from the full recording, but this should not interfere with your listening for the *dō* strokes); start watching the *kuwaheru* pattern in figure 2.13c after that.

- Next focus on each of the other percussion instruments in turn, following the stroke sequences in the notation.

- When you are thoroughly comfortable with the piece through the percussion patterns, shift your listening to the chordophones. Answer this question: Do their parts participate in articulating the metric structure? If so, how?

- Finally, listen to the *shō* part, with the same question in mind.

No doubt you will have noted the slow speed of the selection I have provided. Research has shown that the speed was two to four times as fast in Heian times as it is now. This is certainly suggested by the role of the music in the Heian period. From references in poetry and in diaries written by court women, this elite music was used in conjunction with cock fighting, archery, sumo wrestling, and horseracing, for outdoor entertainment at iris festivals in spring and chrysanthemum festivals in autumn, and at poetry contests. Instrumental ensemble performance (*kangen*) was complemented by dance performance (*bugaku*) and vocal music of several sorts. This music was part of daily life among the nobility. Through the centuries, as the function of the music became more ceremonial, the speed was slowed and the style as a whole became highly ritualized.

ACTIVITY 2.4 *The order in which the instruments enter is always the same in named compositions such as "Etenraku." Listen again to CD track 10 and take note of that order. Compare that order with* netori *performance practice on CD track 8; you can always distinguish a* netori *from a named composition by this difference.*

Without question, "Etenraku" has been the hit tune among *gagaku* compositions. It is performed in three versions, each based on a different *gagaku* melodic mode. The most frequently heard version is in *hyōjō* mode. Indeed, "Etenraku" *hyōjō* has been studied by school children in Japan as the canonized piece of the whole court music repertoire since "a glimpse" of traditional music was put into the public school curriculum in the 1960s. I was not surprised recently to hear it played for a traditional-style wedding at a shrine in Tokyo. "Etenraku" *hyōjō* is also reproduced on numerous commercial recordings. In selecting a piece for this textbook, however, I was interested in widening horizons so I made a compromise: you are becoming familiar with the hit tune, but a version in a different mode (*chō*)—*banshiki*.

GAGAKU THROUGH TIME

Gagaku music has survived as a performed ensemble tradition for nearly a millennium and a half in Japan for, I think, four primary reasons. One is the deep and high cultural prestige it has accrued from its close link with an imperial institution. Another is that that imperial institution has been continuous since the Nara period. Also, the music's function after the Heian period became ceremonial, therefore ritualized, and therefore was gradually transmitted with great care. Finally, it survived because there have consistently been clans of professional court and Buddhist temple musicians who have made it their business to preserve it.

Gagaku music has, however, changed considerably since the Nara period, and what we hear today is the music that it became in the nineteenth century. Change has occurred for numerous reasons, and I can suggest only a few here. From the ninth century the influence of Chinese and other Asian musics gave way to a process of indigenization as Japan turned inward: the number of instruments was reduced, and compositions were transposed into different and fewer modes as modal practice changed. Notation was skeletal at most, with casual reliance on oral and aural transmission until professional musicians focused on potential loss after the Heian period. Then, because the contexts for performance and the degree of patronage began to diminish from the late twelfth century, when the emperor and nobles lost their income to the shogunate, most of the court musicians were dispersed to three temple locations. In isolation from each other, variant performance practices developed. When the three groups were reassembled at the new Imperial Household in Tokyo at the outset of the Meiji period, compromises had to be made in the versions of pieces. (Some of the regathered musicians of the Tokyo palace Music Bureau were the musicians who worked with the Music Study Committee in 1872 to shape music education; staff musicians there were commissioned in 1881 to compose a second "Kimigayo," the song sung today as the national anthem.)

So indigenized has *gagaku* music become in the minds of Japanese that the sense of its foreignness has faded. *Gagaku* is "a representation of the quintessence of Japanese music"(Tanabe and Masu 1953: 16).

In addition, with two exceptions the instrumentarium of the *gagaku* ensemble put into place those very instruments and instrument types that form the core of what became "Japanese traditional music" (*hōgaku*). There could hardly be a more widely ranging result of musical interface with other cultures. The *shō* and *hichiriki* remained distinctively associated with court music until contemporary music began to be written for them in the second half of the twentieth century. *Koto* music, however, took off on a track of its own, becoming the most important instrument for indigenous styles of elite chamber music. The *biwa* became the accompaniment instrument for dramatic storytelling of historic epics such as the *Tales of the Heike*, while the flutes, *taiko, san no tsuzumi,* and *shōko* morphed into various shapes and sizes for folk and theatrical genres.

The two most significant exceptions in the instrumentarium of Japanese *hōgaku*—the *syamisen* (figure 2.14), a long-necked plucked lute, and

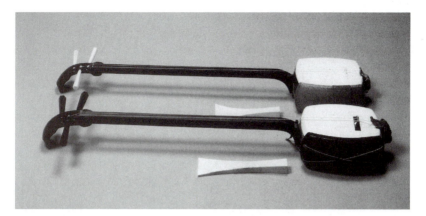

FIGURE 2.14   Syamisen. *Top:* nagauta (kabuki) syamisen; *bottom:* gidayu (bunraku) *syamisen. Ready to be packed up, the long neck is constructed in three sections. The bottom section turns into a spike that enters the box-shaped resonating chamber of the instrument at one end and extends out the far side, thus earning its classification as a spiked lute. The top section ends in the pegbox where three pegs formerly of ivory but now usually of plastic are inserted laterally. The strings of twisted silk run from the pegs, along the unfretted neck, to a tailpiece of silk rope attached to the spike. To achieve the buzzing tonal quality of the competitor* biwa, *in Japan this long-necked lute was modified: the two higher-pitched strings pass over a bridge consisting of a metal ridge at the upper end of the neck; the lowest string is set in a niche in the wooden edge of the pegbox. Immediately below that a slight cavity in the neck allows only the lowest string to vibrate against the wood. The sound box is made of four convex pieces of wood that are carved with patterns inside to improve the sound. The box is closed in on top and bottom by catskin (or dogskin) heads that are pasted on. Since playing is with an ivory or tortoise shell (or plastic or wood) plectrum, the skin in the striking area is reinforced with an extra semicircle of skin.* (Photo by Shinji Aoki.)

the *syakuhati* (figure 2.15), a long bamboo vertical flute, also came from outside Japan, but centuries after the *gagaku* instrumentarium had settled in. I discuss them in the next chapter, as I turn from a primary focus on Japan's interface with international cultures to another theme of the book: a gradual process of popularization.

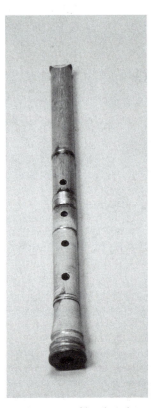

FIGURE 2.15 Syakuhati. *One piece of bamboo that remains almost in its natural form stretches in a straight line from the* utaguchi *(mouth, edge of the blowing end) and then curves gently from the joint below the first hole to the bottom of the instrument. The instrument is made by filing off the roots on that bottom section. Its relationship to the vertical flutes preserved in the Shosoin in Nara or to a later flute (hitoyogiri) introduced possibly around the fifteenth century from China is disputed, but the contemporary* syakuhati *is clearly most closely related in construction to the instrument of the Fuke Zen sect of the Tokugawa era. It differs mostly in the finish applied to the interior that makes the instrument vibrate well, produce a more stable tone, and also play through a higher range (Kitahara et al. 1990:69). Producing a sound on it may take some doing for nonflutists; resting the chin on one side of the tube, one blows down at the opposite side, across an edge created by a piece of water buffalo horn (or some acrylic material) inserted into the cane. The instrument is made in various lengths. (Photo by Shinji Aoki.)*

CHAPTER 3

Focusing Inward and Across Boundaries

∞

In the previous chapter I remarked briefly on the situatedness of Japanese traditional music within the Japanese social and cultural system: each genre of music is clearly associated with some particular group of people and performance context. Certainly *gagaku* is a clear example of that, with its long and continuous association with the imperial establishment and with shrines and temples. In this chapter I explore further the situated nature of several types of traditional music, but with the purpose of pursuing another of the themes of this book—that a process of popularization has occurred in the musical arts through time.

"Popularization" here means music's becoming relatively more accessible to a broader range of people. When this happens through the mass media at the present time, no one questions use of the term "popularization." But I also see it as a useful term for interpreting what has taken place when boundaries of a musical or social nature have been crossed, resulting in a kind of outward mobility that is worthy of note in the Japanese context.

BEYOND CLASSICAL MUSIC TRAINING

To tell the truth, when I first started the Yamaha Music School . . . in May 1954, I didn't have any clear ideas about music popularization. I did feel that it was irresponsible to just sell musical instruments to people without teaching them how to enjoy them (Kawakami 1987: 9)

Inspired by informal music making he observed on trips to Europe and Brazil in 1953, the president of Nippon Gakki (the Yamaha commercial enterprise) began noting that while many Japanese were buying Yamaha reed organs as opposed to pianos, it was rare to walk down a street and hear the sound of one coming out of a house—a natural expectation due to the style of home construction. Thus was founded the nonprofit Yamaha Music School, born of Kawakami's determination to assume the responsibility for teaching people how to enjoy the instruments they purchased: "Opening up the Music School was a social imperative, I thought" (Kawakami 1987: 277). Begun for preschool children in Japan, training initially emphasized the Electone, an early Yamaha organ/synthesizer introduced commercially in 1959:

> At the beginning when we were trying to think up a name for it, we came up with "Electone" because the sound is produced by electricity. At first, it produced a weird sound as if it were broken. . . . But we kept on improving it. Then we used vacuum tubes which heated up and malfunctioned frequently, so the lifetime was short. Then transistors came along, and we used them although they were expensive, and things improved. Yamaha was the first in the world to establish techniques for making sound with transistors. We were also the first in digital sound, and today's semiconductor ICs came out of this. (Kawakami 1987: 276)

Since 1966 the Yamaha Music Foundation has been devoted to the promotion of music popularization, self-consciously moving education in music beyond formal individual and music school training. With instruction now extended to all ages in numerous countries and many instruments, the focus remains on popular rather than classical music. The aim is to provide students a good foundation in "TDS" (tonic, dominant, and subdominant chords) and a well-cultivated sense of pitch, thereby giving them the facility to compose their own melodies and to improvise.

> Some music for the synchronized swimming in this Olympics [1984] was written by JOC children [performers in the annual Junior Original Concert], and the Canadian ice skating music was written by JOC children from Nagoya. . . . Emi Watanabe, the figure skater, also used music by the Yamaha children. (Kawakami 1987: 270)

BEYOND THE PALACE

Smiling out at me from a larger-than-life-sized poster at the Yamano store on the Ginza in downtown Tokyo in 2001, the representation of Hideki Togi lured me in: I could not resist joining thousands of Japanese in buying CDs of his "feel-good" compositions (as the bins containing his recordings were labeled that year). The eerie, ritualized sound of the *hichiriki* has turned soothing, somehow relaxing and reassuring.

> I just make music that feels good to me. I'm not particularly concerned with the question of genres, of *gagaku* versus Western music. Still, even when I create new music I am always aware of *gagaku's* special place in my heart. To me *gagaku* itself is the perfect form of artistic expression. (*Nipponia* 1998: cover interview)

Having heard from friends about his extravagant live productions, I also purchased videos that bring *gagaku* face to face with global popular culture.

Hideki Togi (b. 1959), an Imperial Household *hichiriki* player from a hereditary family of court musicians, completed the traditional ten-year period of training, then headed for a different career. His productions provide an otherworldly yet very worldly juxtaposition of reenactments of Heian period music making and dance with his own compositions. Picture this: in one video (Togi 2000), truer to Heian period practice than court practice today, we see women as well as men clothed in gorgeous Heian period dress, forming an ensemble that spreads out on both sides of an enormous stage under a dramatic full-moon stage setting. Crickets fill the soundscape before they play, setting us in romantic nature and, for Japanese listeners, evoking the feeling of the summer season. Togi is at the center, playing first one of the *gagaku* instruments then another, with the help of polished film editing. In another segment the solo dancer in fantastic *bugaku* costume is none other than Togi himself; with the camera focused in a close-up on the character's mask, with breathtaking rapidity we suddenly see the face of Togi himself, then again the mask. The "feel-good music" that follows on the video, with a meditative turtleneck-clad Togi playing *hichiriki* over a lush accompaniment of an assortment of Japanese and Western instruments, is probably what brings in his huge audiences. Pop production par excellence, it is introducing Japanese youth to the ancient tradition with an incredible mixture of historic performance practice and kitch. But introducing it he is, to a very wide audience that would probably never have experienced that significant part of Japanese musical history otherwise.

In fact, community *gagaku* ensembles are popping up in many places, taught mostly by former court musicians. Most distinguished among the musicians is Sukeyasu Shiba (b. 1935), who is also composing for the whole ensemble. Heard in concert beyond the palace and on CD by the superb non-court group Reigakusha, which he directs, there are now numerous new pieces from within the tradition for the first time in a very long time.

Among the earliest of the *gagaku* instruments to be adopted for purposes beyond the palace was the *biwa*. Its function as the instrument for self-accompanying by storytellers on the southern island of Kyushu from the twelfth to thirteenth centuries put it squarely in the sphere of popular culture. Best-known among their stories is the martial epic *Tales of the Heike*, which recounts the dramatic struggle for power between the Heike clan (the Taira family) and the Genji clan (the Minamoto family) of the *samurai* (warrior) class that ultimately resulted in the founding of the Kamakura Shogunate (1185–1333; see chapter 4).

The instrument itself was indigenized, according to an aesthetic value in Japanese music: noise, in addition to more purposefully "musical" sound, is incorporated into the desired sound. In Japan the *biwa* was modified to produce an effect called *sawari* (literally, "touch"). The bridges are intentionally higher, thereby loosening the strings to create ambiguous pitches or a "noisy" sound. One pluck produces sound that is so complex harmonically that one's listening should be concentrated more on the sound itself than on a melodic phrase in which it is embedded (CD track 11). *Sawari*, and also the percussive sound of the larger plectrum hitting the wooden body of the instrument, are just two examples of how "noise" is incorporated into the sound aesthetic of Japanese traditional music. The noise in *biwa* musical practice also serves to heighten the dramatic effect of the instrument's use in accompanying recitation of martial tales.

More recently, taking the *biwa* into yet another musical sphere, the composer Toru Takemitsu (1930–96) scored his "Eclipse" (1966) and later his famous piece "November Steps" (1967) (CD track 11; see below) for *biwa* and *syakuhati*. While he was by no means the first composer to score contemporary music for traditional instruments, Takemitsu's referencing of "Japaneseness" by calling for traditional instruments and by drawing on the artistry of distinguished musicians from the traditional music world caused an international sensation.

Like the music he created, Takemitsu's career developed beyond the boundaries of academic education in European music that was and is far more likely to characterize the path of a Japanese composer of contemporary music. Born in Tokyo, he spent the first seven years of his life in China, where his father was employed. By 1947, two years after the end of World War II, the eighteen-year-old had already decided to follow the difficult road to becoming a composer, thereby losing him his family's support but also, I think, freeing him. Avoiding regular schooling, he worked in the dining room of an American military base of the Occupation Forces. From that time the piano became a particularly meaningful instrument to him; at the base he was allowed to use a Yamaha grand piano. When the base was closed, he rented a Pleyal piano, which produced sounds that suited his developing admiration for French composers. Takemitsu's public debut as a composer came on 7 December 1950 with "Lento in due movimenti" for piano. He was subsequently supported by other composers but was essentially self-taught. Takemitsu is usually credited with organizing the Experimental Workshop, a then-radical but influential group that supported collaborative activities in multiple artistic media. To earn a living he (and a number of other composers) wrote for film, radio, and theater.

For Takemitsu, composing for film (completing ninety-three scores) became a way of life that made him the best-known composer in Japan. When asked why he chose to write so extensively for the cinema, he responded that he loved the movies and "the reason I love movies is because I experience them as music." He found films to be a way "into the outside," "like getting a visa to freedom" (notes, CD Nonesuch/Film 79404-2, *The Film Music of Toru Takemitsu*).

BEYOND THE TEMPLE

"Do you know that the ultimate achievement the *shakuhachi* master strives for in his performance is the re-creation of the sound of wind blowing through an old bamboo grove?" (Takemitsu 1995: 87–88). Such is the aesthetic that connects the *syakuhati* (CD tracks 11 and 12) with Zen, a form of Buddhism that takes seriously humankind's connection with nature and also techniques of meditation, including the use of music as a means to enlightenment.

While the history of Zen is clearly traceable to China, the history of the Fuke sub-sect of Zen is considerably less clear. A loosely organized fraternity of *syakuhati*-playing beggar minstrels is known to have existed in the late Ashikaga period (1336–1573). In the Tokugawa period (1600–1868) membership in the fraternity swelled owing to the entry of large numbers of *rōnin*, relatively well educated men of the high *samurai* class who, after responsible careers as the vassals of powerful lords who were defeated by the Tokugawa clan, suddenly found themselves masterless and living lives of little purpose. Transformed into a serious sub-sect of Zen early in the Tokugawa era, members (called *komusō*) were required to learn to play the *syakuhati*.

Three important Fuke religious sites developed—two near Edo and one in Kyoto, noticeably near the political centers. In applying for government license, a "history" of the sect was "documented" that justified its musical tradition: Pu-ko, the famous Zen eccentric of Tang China (who, we are told, was one of the wisest men of his time) "liked to play the role of a madman and run through the streets ringing a bell. Toward the end of the founder Pu-ko's life, a Zen-oriented admirer, Chang Po, managed to 'capture' the ineffable, non-verbal, transforming essence of Pu-ko's hand-bell and play it on the flute. He called this flute tune the 'Hollow bell' or 'Empty bell' since the flute was hollow" (Sanford 1977: 416). Thus was the sound of a ringing bell mapped on to the *syakuhati*. In 1614 Ieyasu, the founder of the Tokugawa shogunate, bestowed a special charter upon the *komusō* that in effect gave that military government a means of controlling a large group of *rōnin*. The charter granted them unique privileges, including a monopoly over the playing of the *syakuhati*, and also the right of wearing an identity-obscuring basket hat down over the face—in Buddhist terms, a sign of humility, but if misused, an opportunity to hide or to spy.

The Fuke musical repertoire came to comprise two categories of pieces. The *honkyoku* ("original," or "fundamental pieces") were those explicitly connected to Zen and the temple traditions. Among them were Chang Po's "Empty Bell" and also "Longing for the Bell" (CD track 12). The other category consisted of *gaikyoku* ("outside pieces"), pieces played with the *koto* and *syamisen*, a frequent occurrence in the Edo period in the secular money-making endeavors of the schools of *syakuhati* instruction.

In the course of the Tokugawa period, the paths of the Fuke centers diverged. The temple in Kyoto became deeply religious, the result perhaps of the lack of political power in that imperial city as well as the commitment to tradition in that region of the country. In Edo, however, the control of the Fuke sect over *syakuhati* playing was weakened by the establishment of schools of instruction separate from the temples. Kinko Kurosawa (ca. 1705–71), the monk responsible for that, traveled around the country collecting *syakuhati* music, which he compiled and edited as a thirty-six-piece repertory. A progressive shift from religious instrument to more secular and popular was underway.

As the end of the Tokugawa period neared, incidences of misbehavior on the part of *samurai komusō* and misuse of the heavy end of the instrument became increasingly problematic. Its role in popular culture is depicted in figure 1.4, a woodblock print in the *ukiyo-e* style, depicting characters and scenes from the popular *kabuki* theater. In 1871, shortly after the beginning of the Meiji era, the Fuke sect of Zen was abolished, along with professional guilds of all sorts, in the interest of modernizing the nation.

Serious players of *syakuhati*, among them disciples in the teaching line of Kinko Kurosawa and also players in the Kyoto style, pursued other means of livelihood with their instrument. Teaching groups (*ryū*) formed through them and others, notation for *syakuhati* repertoire was created, and the organization of the tradition developed into its present-day form. The Kyoto group came to be known as the Myōan *ryū*. Described as "ethereal," the style of their music retained a meditative aura, emphasizing long phrases and also extravagant variations in speed and strength that suggest sudden insight; it can even be improvisational—a rarity in Japanese traditional music.

The Kinko *ryū* actively pursued ensemble playing of traditional-style compositions with *koto* and *syamisen* players in an ensemble practice known still as *sankyoku* ("three pieces," here meaning three instruments; CD track 13). Essentially complementing the *koto* (or *syamisen*) melody in the heterophonic texture of the *sankyoku* performing practice, the *syakuhati* serves musically to sustain the pitches, whereas the sounds of the *koto* and *syamisen* strings die away quickly. Playing the *syakuhati* also provided culturally aspiring middle-class men an opportunity to participate in relatively elitist and entirely secular chamber music.

Jumping forward in time for a moment, I want to cite Christopher Yohmei Blasdel, an accomplished American *syakuhati* player who lives in Japan and who provides excellent insight into the *iemoto seito*, a traditional system for transmission of knowledge between master and disciple. All of us who have studied an instrument in Japan (for me, *koto* and *syamisen*) will recognize the process. He describes his instruction from the master artist Goro Yamaguchi in a way that puts the *honkyoku* and *gaikyoku* repertoires in perspective.

> Mondays were lesson days. . . . The pattern was the same: I arrived [at his house], awaited my turn, then played through the day's lesson with the teacher. After playing through once, Yamaguchi sang the *shakuhachi* part while I played alone. He corrected mistakes in rhythm or fingering, and particularly difficult passages he repeated with me several times. In the more advanced pieces, I found it exceedingly difficult to keep up with his pace. I often felt overwhelmed and, when I fell behind, exasperated. Even then, however, Yamaguchi

continued playing the piece until the end of the section. I later realized that playing the piece through, even with mistakes, provided a sense of flow and unity. It also helped to bring the piece into the body, rather than remaining as an intellectual exercise.

The lessons, although demanding, were the highpoint of the week. Sitting in front of him for a few minutes every week was more than just a music lesson. Yamaguchi's intensely powerful, beautiful sound stimulated and relaxed me, becoming a kind of therapy which was much more effective than any kind of counseling and more potent than any drug or sensual pleasure. Walking back to the station after one of his lessons, I invariably felt tremendous inspiration and relief. . . .

The pieces one learns in *shakuhachi* lessons have a set order. After the basic exercises and simple practice songs, the beginning student starts right away learning the classical repertoire: *Kuro Kami, Roku Dan no Shirabe* or *Chidori no Kyoku*. These are termed *gaikyoku*, or "outside pieces" since they are almost all music with song—based on the rich literary traditions of Japan—written originally for the *koto* or *shamisen* and are "outside" the original *shakuhachi* repertoire. The beginner is expected to learn about 74 of these pieces (also called *sankyoku*); a commitment of about six years. It is only after the student has mastered these pieces that they can proceed to the heart of *shakuhachi* music: the lofty solo *honkyoku* compositions.

Six years might seem a long time to spend on pieces which are outside the *shakuhachi* repertory, but there are reasons for this. First of all, spending several years on these pieces insures that the student has mastered the considerable technical aspects of the instrument and music, but it also provides the student with a skill; that of accompanying song, *koto* and *shamisen* and learning the subtleties of ensemble playing. . . .

. . . It took me some time to realize the nature of the relationship between the teacher (*sensei*) and the student (*seito*) in Japan [i.e., the *iemoto* system]. It is not a relationship based on money paid per hour of instruction. Rather, one pays for the privilege of belonging to the group of students which gather around the teacher. In Yamaguchi's case, this group is known as the Chikumei-sha. My monthly *gessha* [payment for instruction] admitted me into that group, and loyalty to the group was expected. Group loyalty is, of course, very important in the Japanese society, but sometimes I thought that the independent nature of the *shakuhachi*—an instrument so superbly fitted to solo performance—was contradictory with group-oriented activities.

The group maintained itself in a rigid hierarchy, with, of course, Yamaguchi at the peak. I, at the very bottom, was at first unaware of my duties and responsibilities to the group and made more than my share of mistakes and breaches of etiquette. I was fortunate that Yamaguchi was forgiving of these mistakes and my youthful ignorance. . . .

Aspects of the money flow between teacher and student in the teacher's *iemoto* guild system remained unclear to me for some time. The monthly lesson fees were simple enough to understand, but I soon discovered that there were other fees involved, for example, the entry fee and a "progress fee" as the student passed certain stages in the *shakuhachi* repertory. The *gaikyoku* pieces were divided into four levels of increasing difficulty. When a student finished a certain level, they are awarded a certificate. . . .

The ultimate level or final "graduation" is when all the pieces, both *gaikyoku* and *honkyoku*, are learned and the student is granted a performing license, called *shihan*, and performing name. Receiving a name from the teacher signifies considerable expense, but with it comes social recognition as an official teacher of the teacher's *iemoto* guild. As a beginning foreign student, I could hardly imagine ever paying out so much money or reaching such heights, nor did I understand the necessity to "pay one's dues" in order to fully belong to the Japanese society.

Some traditional Japanese performing arts require a tremendous outlay of money. *Koto* and *shamisen* lesson fees, for example, tend to be high, but in addition the student must purchase expensive instruments and accessories. Many *iemoto* guilds in the traditional performing arts hold regular student recitals, whose considerable costs—hall rentals, publicity, performance fees for the accompanying musicians, etc.—must be borne entirely by the students. Depending on the guild and the fame of the teacher, a student can pay tens of thousands of dollars just to go through the system and receive a professional name. . . .

The worlds of Japanese dance and theater tend to cost even more. . . .

. . . I was lucky to have chosen a traditional Japanese instrument that was relatively cheap and easy to carry around. I was even more fortunate to have found a patient teacher who tolerated my ignorance and kept showing me how intriguingly beautiful *shakuhachi* music could be. (Blasdel 1990: 17–26, cited with permission of the author)

ACTIVITY 3.1 *In the* honkyoku, *characteristics of traditional* syakuhati *music can be heard best. In CD track 12, an excerpt from "Reibo" ("Longing for the Bell," Shoganken Temple version) is performed by the late Kinko* ryū *artist Kifu Mitsuhashi.*

Listen first to the passage of the melody through time, then answer these questions.

- Do you hear 'pulsation at any point? If so, at what timing in the selection?

- Do you have a sense of breathing rhythm, such as you hear in *gagaku netori?* Persons who do hear it connect this music with meditation and spirituality. The rhythm of the piece potentially varies from playing to playing.

- Can you predict how long a phrase will be, i.e., when the player will take a breath, thereby creating a unit of melody?

- Now focus on the spaces (*ma*) between melodic units. Are they just dead moments of silence or merely a chance to take a breath? Or do you hear the spaces as meaningful to the overall effect of the music?

- Listen for the qualities of sound that are being produced on the instrument. Does the timbre change—at one point soft and breathy, at another point a clearer sound, for instance? If you hear different timbres, take note of the timings.

Think about this famous Zen dictum, "Enlightenment through one tone," as you listen for the ways Mitsuhashi-sensei treats each pitch. Do you hear any of these melodic details beyond the occurrence I have noted?

- An ornamental dip down to the next pitch below, then back up (at 0:23, 0:29–31, for instance)

- A slur connecting two pitches (at 0:01, 0:36, for instance)

- An approach from a pitch above or below to a pitch that will be sustained (1:27)

- A subtle increase or decrease of volume as a pitch is sustained (0:08–15)

- A quick ornamental flip to the pitch above during a sustained pitcy (0:14, 0:52, for instance)
- A sudden burst of sound (0:44)

Kifu Mitsuhashi studied with both Kinko ryū and Meian ryū teachers. He has won prestigious awards as a performer of both traditional and contemporary syakuhati music, and has commissioned a number of pieces from noted Japanese composers.

Further popularization of the *syakuhati* was assured in 1896 when the Tozan *ryū* was founded in Osaka by Tozan Nakao (1876–1956). Tozan was an ambitious musician who decided to become a force in the country's process of modernization by moving the *syakuhati* closer to the sphere of international music and specifically that of the West. Adapting the *syakuhati* vertical notation to the five-line staff, he yielded in his compositions to the sense of rhythmic organization in Western meter with strong beat patterns and advocated the concept of a piece as a fixed rather than a relatively flexible item. An organized individual, he founded schools throughout the country; he was utterly in step with the spirit of early twentieth-century Japan.

At present each group of *syakuhati* players (almost exclusively men) has its repertoire of pieces—*honkyoku* and *gaikyoku*—and styles of playing remain somewhat distinctive. The connection to Zen, the discipline of learning to play a difficult instrument, attraction to an almost yogic concentration, and control of breathing as a form of meditation remain a part of the experience of *syakuhati* for some players, especially those who are American. The playing of the *honkyoku* continues in that spirit. Through its long life beyond the temples, the *syakuhati* became and continues to be one of the most popular of Japanese instruments for chamber music.

FUZZING OF FOLK AND POPULAR

Tsugaru Syamisen. The long line waiting at Orchard Hall in Tokyo on 12 May 2003 finally disappeared as fans of the Yoshida Kyodai (brothers) took their seats. The attraction of the music of the young brothers Ryoichiro (then age twenty-five) and Ken-ichi (then age twenty-two) Yoshida for all variety of people was astounding. Their audience comprised parents with children just old enough to be permitted in, nattily dressed teens, mid-aged sophisticates, senior citizens—and one American ethnomusicologist. The stage setting was simple, with a small platform for each brother and risers behind for a few other performers; the dramatic lighting effects of a typical pop concert were yet to come. Striding onstage in traditional dress (in contrast with their mod hairstyles), the brothers were greeted with a roar of anticipation; then we settled in to hear selections that went in and out of the distinctive traditional music of the Tsugaru region in the snow country of northern Honshu Island.

> Sometimes we are accompanied by other types of instruments, like Japanese drums or percussion instruments from Peru, and we use rhythms you wouldn't hear in traditional Japanese folksongs. That's why our music is often labeled unorthodox, even more so than that of other *tsugaru-jamisen* [*syamisen*] players. We're carrying on the old traditions, but if we don't introduce new elements, young people will not be interested in our music. And our audience certainly like what we do." (cited in Tsuchiya 2002: 3).

Indeed, they (and I) do! In 2001 the Yoshidas won Album of the Year in the "traditional Japanese music" category at the fifteenth Japan Gold Disc awards. CD track 14 gives you a quick hint of the dynamic, percussive style of this music, with its fast triple rhythmic feel. The tip of the plectrum is thin to produce a sharp sound when hitting the string and the skin almost simultaneously; percussive effects—noise—are a significant part of this and other *syamisen* styles. Whereas the Tsugaru tradition also includes soulful, ornamental vocal music, the Yoshida Kyodai show off their considerable instrumental virtuosity, offering instrumental versions of songs (popular and folk, international and Japanese) but also the melodic yet competitive improvisational style that appeals to Japanese who are enculturated to expectations for individual soloistic virtuosity.

The Syamisen. By way of the Ryukyu Islands (now Okinawa), an instrument related to the Chinese *san-hsien* was introduced to Japan around the 1560s; it, too, is evidence of Japan's interface with Asian neighbors. A much lighter, more portable plucked lute, the *syamisen* challenged the role of the more cumbersome *biwa* as accompaniment for storytellers, the preeminent popular musicians/raconteurs of the time. Its popularity immediately spread, adopted by blind wandering beggars such as the ancestors of the Tsugaru style, and by singers of

FIGURE 3.1   *"A Puppet Show: The Story of the Potted Trees," a six-panel screen. Japanese* bungaku. *Edo period, eighteenth century. Freer Gallery of Art, Smithsonian Institution, Washington, D.C.* (Gift of Charles Lang Freer. (F198.505).)

Buddhist ballads and diverse styles of folk and popular song. It became the primary instrument for the *bunraku* (puppet) theater (figure 3.1) and *kabuki* theater (see chapter 4). Commonplace as well in the pleasure districts of major cities, it was part of the fabric of urban culture from the sixteenth century. In reading the history, it seems that wherever there has been popular musical entertainment, there has been the *syamisen*. Seeming more like "classical" genres today, as traditional music has been edged into corners of Japanese life by Western music, a number of those popular styles remain in performance.

The *syamisen* used for different performance genres differ somewhat, but features in common make them look similar (figure 2.14). They differ in the thickness of the neck and the size of the box; *syamisen* used for Tsugaru-*jamisen* and music in the puppet theater (*bunraku*) are the largest. A middle-sized neck is used in chamber music (*jiuta-sokyoku* compositions, CD track 13), while the thinnest is used for music of the *kabuki* theater and more "popular" song forms. Instruments differ also in the length of the neck (Tsugaru-*jamisen* being the longest at three feet), thickness of the skin that closes in the sound box, thickness of the strings, shape of the plectrum used to play it, and—most telling for differences in sound—the type of bridge that is used to hold the strings above the sound box and neck. With a bridge whose backside (facing the skin) has been carved out to make thin walls combined with a particular placement of plectrum striking, the *syamisen* sound in *nagauta* is also percussive (CD track 15).

The construction of the *syamisen* is not as standardized as, for instance, the thirteen-stringed *koto*. Even among players within one tradition (musical style and repertoire) there is not necessarily complete standardization (Philip Flavin, personal communication, 2001). What might seem like minor differences are important to players who have committed themselves to learning a particular style and repertoire from a particular teacher who favors a particular instrument. Thus is the world of *syamisen* organized.

Most "*syamisen* music" is actually *syamisen*-accompanied song (CD track 7), whether lyrical or narrative; soloistic instrumental music such as Tsugaru-*jamisen* and compositions now being written by contemporary composers are the exceptions. Not surprisingly, then, relatively few playing techniques are used on the *syamisen*. Up and down stroking is very common, producing a pattern spoken as "*chiri kara.*" Left-hand plucking and stopping of a string also occur. Glissandos are produced by sliding the left hand along the neck on a string depressed by one of the fingers of the right hand. Tsugaru-*jamisen* players exploit the different sounds achieved from striking the strings higher or lower along the neck. Nuance can be important, however, such as the difference in timbre when a pitch is repeated on a different string. The lack of frets to mark the position of pitches makes this long-necked lute challenging to play.

Drumming Ensembles. Drums in Japan—many sizes, many shapes, many contexts, many purposes. This comes as no surprise to anyone, thanks to a percussion phenomenon known as *taiko* (generically, "drum"). Slightly more specifically, *kumi daiko* (any collection of drums and other percussion instruments for an ensemble) was the basis for a "new tradition" that originated in America with Seiichi Tanaka, the Japanese-American founder in 1968 of the San Francisco Taiko Dojo. While Tanaka studied with particular teachers in Japan, he also understood that *kumi daiko* has always been local—many styles and many purposes. Thus he felt free to develop *taiko* in America in his own way—into highly choreographed movement to produce compelling percussive rhythms. One search on the Internet for "*taiko dojo*" will show you how powerfully successful Tanaka has been.

That *taiko* is a major element in Japanese diaspora is further attested to by the numerous organizations for it throughout North America and elsewhere. I witnessed this in Japan in 1999 when a major shopping mall built by foreigners was opened by a female *taiko* group composed largely of Americans, led by a Japanese woman. Talk about gender and "the local" in an era of globalization!

Perhaps you have heard of Ondekoza, the Japanese group that took the idea of physical movement and drumming to a high level (CD track 16). Founded as a community in 1969 on Sado Island in the Sea of Japan, the group—young men and women who had no previous association with traditional arts—took inspiration from a local Sado "demon drum" tradition and took as their name the term for the powerful sound of drums in the local dialect (*ondeko*). With long-distance running as the means to build their physical and mental fitness for drumming, they established a reputation in the global popular music world by combining concerts with runs. Most spectacular was the 9,500-mile run around the perimeter of the United States, starting on 12 November 1990 with a concert in Carnegie Hall (New York City) and ending the same way on 3 December 1993. Like the American *taiko dojo*, the idea and the music originate from folk music and traditional festival drum routines played on bamboo flutes, stringed instruments, and drums of various sizes.

In Japan, drumming has more commonly functioned in other ways, many of them related to spiritual practice: priests in Shinto shrines drumming to banish evil spirits, drumming to communicate with and entertain the spirits, drumming the "voice" of Buddha, celebrating the harvest and other agricultural rites linked to the spirits of nature. The Tokyo *taiko* instructor who led the previously-mentioned female group, Mokoko Igarashi (MI in the quotation below), spoke with me (BW) about its link to local life (14 April 1999).

MI: These kinds of traditions have almost disappeared from everywhere in Japan.

BW: You mean *taiko* is not being done in the countryside?

MI: Right, right. In the old time when there were more farmers, more fishermen, you know, there were more festivals for the harvest. When you come to my class, I'll show you how the *taiko* movements are from the movement of workers. Like when they do the rice planting, they have a basket here [she does the motion for me] and they have to move up and down, up and down to put in the small plant. So that movement is the same as Japanese dance and Japanese drumming. When fishermen go to sea, they have to throw the net, so we have in the dance the exact same movement. Especially in the northern part of Japan, it's like a treasure—many different dances and drumming. It's not for the higher-status people—it's completely for local people.

BW: Now when you say that they do *taiko*, do they actually still farm with drumming?

MI: No, actually in the village it's just for pleasure. For *taiko*, you know, there are many different styles for performing. According to the area, like the Tokyo area and the northern area, they are very different. Even how to put the *taiko* on the stand is different. I like the style from the northern part because it's more direct.

BW: Are there different styles within an area—within Tokyo, for example?

MI: Yes, for the Sanja *matsuri*, held in Asakusa [area of Tokyo], for instance. It's one of three most famous festivals in Japan.

Asakusa is a typical place for *matsuri*, and they have a spirit, or *iki*. They feel they are very different from any other people in Japan or even other Tokyo areas. They don't see the things directly—a little bit slanted. And they need to be very elegant, like the way they play *taiko*. They don't hit the *taiko* up and down. They have to put the *taiko* on the stand this way [slanting at an angle from the ground], and they play from the side. Now in most of Tokyo, the *taiko* will be slanted on the stand.

Then they don't hit the front; they stay beside the *taiko* and put themselves in . . . like a capital L. The right hand comes like this [demonstrating], but the left is like a back hand, so they have to cross the arms every time they hit. To really get this form, it takes time, right? Because you have to move right and left in a very different way. Then you always look at your left shoulder in a slanted way; you don't look at the things directly. The audience is over there [indicating].

The way I learned in the northern part of Japan, it's very straight. Put the *taiko* even on the floor, the top is a little bit up, but the very important thing is up and down, up and down [demonstrating all the while]. So when you hit the *taiko* down, you have no tension. Then you must have very strong waist and legs for support. This is important for farmers and fishermen because the movement comes from their work.

Then, along with this up-and-down movement, also you have left foot front and right foot back. This is like a fisherman. You have to know the fisherman's song from Hokkaido, "Soran bushi." They have to row. They have to slide their body from back to forward—this movement. This also we have in *taiko* performance. You have to slide yourself forward—back and forth, so basically there are two movements—up and down, and then back and forth

BW: Here in Tokyo are there competitions or anything like that?

MI: There is no competition, but there are many festivals. There is a Japan Taiko Association. We have to pay a lot of money to be a member. And they have a concert—big festival once a year. For adult and then children.

BW: So would you say that *taiko* is having a boom here in the urban area?

MI: I think boom in the world! Because in the paper, an article said that there are more than 150 groups in northern America—Canada and America. Don't you think this is amazing? And I'm sure that many groups don't include any Japanese. Like Japanese American, Chinese American, or Korean American. Personally I think it is very good that the *taiko* is a Japanese instrument, but beat is from all over the world, you know. Like African beat. So they hit the *taiko* and they have their own rhythm from their culture.

BW: Then what makes it *taiko*?

MI: I think spirit, spirit still. Spirit. Because when I studied European percussion, technique was very important. But I never moved up and down and I never obviously expressed myself. I expressed myself through the instrument. But *taiko* is . . . we can actually say music but also like physical activity. You need to use the entire body and we think the energy starts from the earth. Underground. That maybe the energy comes from god, through the earth and then through the earth, the energy comes from your body, and then after the energy goes through your body and then finally comes out through the sticks. So then the energy is circulating; it's not just the technique, you know. That's very interesting.

Matsuri Bayashi.   As you could "hear" from Mokoko-san above and in the description of the Kanamura *matsuri* in chapter 1, a sense of local tradition pervades festivals. At Asakusa, one of the first areas to be developed in Tokyo, its Shinto shrine and Buddhist Kannon Temple have been the locus of festivals and fairs for many centuries, and the area around it has been a thriving entertainment hub in the city, with traditional theaters and other places of amusement. Even now, when Asakusa is a staid, quiet business area by comparison, pockets of very old houses survive and the area comes alive with festivities such as the famous Sanja festival held by the Asakusa shrine every year in May (the festival referenced in CD track 7). Decorative paper lanterns and employees in traditional outfits greet the crowds arriving at the Asakusa subway station on the Ginza line. Daytime shopping and eating occur at tiny shops along the *nakamise*, a narrow "street" created by parallel lines of open-fronted shops, off which radiate several arcade streets at the approach to the Kannon temple. When evening comes and hundreds of lanterns are lit, however, excitement mounts in anticipation of the procession of more than one thousand participants in festival gear supporting portable shrines lacquered and shining with gold. Through the streets they come, under the old Kaminari gate, down the *nakamise*, to the shrine.

Behind the portable shrines comes the music of instrumental ensembles, *matsuri bayashi* on parade. The men carrying each heavy portable shrine are likely to be parishioners of a shrine, but the musicians in any of the one hundred or so neighborhoods in the Asakusa area are just "people." For the Sanja festival, each ensemble—five members strong, male or female, younger or older, playing a flute, a small metal gong, and three drums—has convened in a neighborhood to practice once a week for several weeks leading up to the festival, then nightly as the date approaches. An older man will teach the others orally and visually; in the spirit of farmers' music, there is little incentive to modernize and notate (with exceptions, of course). So embedded in the fabric of communities are these *hayashi* that room rent is suspended for the practice sessions in cultural centers or shops (Catherine Ochi, personal communication, 16 May 2002).

As in every other Japanese traditional music, there are multiple styles and diverse repertoire of rhythms and melodies among the groups; local traditions remain strong even in the cities. Three evenings a week, children and youths gather at Toshio Osawa's house in Koganei, in the western part of Tokyo, to learn *nukui-bayashi,* a style of music and dance for the Nukui shrine festival developed in the first half of the nineteenth century. It died out after World War II but has been revived by Osawa himself based on the Meguro school of *hayashi*. It is all very local.

> The children start dancing to the music with exaggerated movements, keeping their center of gravity low. Right now they are imitating farmers in old Japan, using hoes to turn over the soil, wringing their sweat out of their hand towels. Later, during a formal performance, they'll wear masks, becoming a lion jester, moonfaced woman, lion, fox or other creature. . . . (figure 3.2) Osawa explains, "The best thing about *hayashi* music and dance is that everyone can join in. When the mood rises toward a climax, people in the audience find themselves dancing, too. (Torikai, 2002: 18)

A *nukui-bayashi* performance has five male or female musicians playing traditional instruments. I list them here in order of entrance on CD track 17: two small barrel-shaped drums mounted together slightly slanted in a low frame, flute and hand-held gong, and a large barrel-shaped drum resting on a low frame. The terms for the same instru-

FIGURE 3.2 Matsuri bayashi. *Ninba dance with distorted masks, for the* sabura matsuri. *Behind the dancers from left to right:* Ōdo *(drum),* kane *(gong), two* tsuke-daiko *(drums),* fue *(flute).* (*Photo by Tatsuko Takizawa.*)

ments vary widely, so here I shall just speak about them as types. The flutist plays patterns that he or she varies and ornaments with numerous repetitions. Just as you saw in *gagaku*, the percussionists play coordinated patterns, but all know that the flutist will coordinate at pertinent moments as well. Signals are given by *kakegoe* (calls by a drummer).

ACTIVITY 3.2 *Figure 3.3 gives you a pattern called "Ninba" that is part of a much longer piece called "Yatai." (*Matsuri bayashi *being very local and therefore very variable, you can find other versions of "Yatai" on different recordings. The patterns here are those of Osawa's* nukui-bayashi*). Strokes are spoken with mnemonic syllables for learning, as follows.*

The syllable "*su*" indicates silence (a rest).

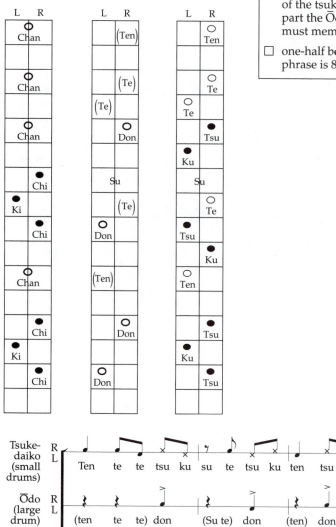

FIGURE 3.3 Nukui-bayashi *pattern "Ninba" from "Yatai"* *(Courtesy of Toshio Osawa and Tatsuko Takizawa, Aichi University of Education.)*

Large drum (*ōdo*): the player sits facing one of the two heads and hits it squarely, "*don*," with left or right hand stick.

Small drums (*tsuke-daiko*): Two players sit facing the two shallow drums, each with two sticks; the two are at different pitch levels. The "*ten*" (or if played rapidly, "*te*") is a real hit, and "*tsu*" (or, if two of these are played in quick succession, "*tsu ku*"), a light touch.

Gong (*kane*): Holding the gong with one hand and stick in the other, a clear hit on the center that is permitted to ring is "*chan*," while a hit on the side that is damped with fingers of the hand that holds the gong is "*chi*" (or, if two are played in succession, "*chi ki*").

With at least two friends, speak each of the patterns in figure 3.3 until you are all comfortable with them. Then split them up among you and speak them together. Figure 3.3 gives you the patterns for left and right hand, so you can also try them physically.

For all Japanese, the music of the *matsuri bayashi* is unmistakable. Referenced in other performance genres from chamber music to theater, it recalls simultaneously a sense of tradition and the memory of some recent fun.

WITHIN THE WORLD OF *KOTO*

In 2002 the Grand Prize in Music from the Japanese Ministry of Culture was awarded to Keiko Nosaka (b. 1938), a musician whose career has spanned the worlds of traditional and contemporary, indigenous and internationalized Japanese music (figures 3.4 and 3.5). On CD track 18 you can hear her playing on a modernized *koto* of her creation. Through Nosaka, I shall delve into the organization of the *koto* world and the gradual popularization of music for the instrument.

Keiko Nosaka and the Twenty-stringed Koto.   Nosaka grew up with *hōgaku* training at home from her late mother, Soju Nosaka (d. 2002), the *iemoto* (head) of a traditional group of *koto* and *syamisen* players. Like all Japanese children, she had European music training at school. Then, the teaching of *koto* took place at her home, as mostly fe-

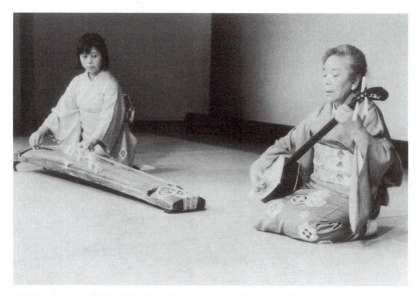

FIGURE 3.4 *Keiko Nosaka (thirteen-stringed* koto*) and her mother,* iemoto *Soju Nosaka (*jiuta syamisen*). Note the finger picks on K. Nosaka's right hand.* (Photo courtesy of Keiko Nosaka.)

male students came for instruction once a week, or more, or less. Lessons were a social as well as musical experience in the years her mother still taught, as the number of pairs of shoes shed at the entryway would indicate (for cleanliness, shoes are not worn indoors in a Japanese home). In whatever order they might arrive on the designated teaching day, however long they wished to stay, all gathered in the *tatami* (straw mat flooring) room, listening to each other's lessons, sipping tea, enjoying the sense of community. Some teachers maintain this to the present; Nosaka does so with her mother's students but not with her own, owing to her busy performing life.

Some aspects of the whole system of *koto* instruction in Japan have not changed, however. While many of the female students want to achieve just enough to make them attractive for a good marriage, serious students learn to play more of the group's repertoire and some attain certification from the *iemoto* to become teachers themselves. Like students of *syakuhati*, most *koto* students play in an annual public recital before an audience of relatives and friends, although it costs a great deal of money.

FIGURE 3.5 *Keiko Nosaka playing the twenty-five-stringed* koto *with string ensemble.* *(Photo courtesy of Keiko Nosaka.)*

In 1963 Keiko Nosaka finished the "Special Study" course at the Tokyo National University of Fine Arts and Music (known in Japan as Geidai), with a degree equivalent to a Master of Fine Arts in the American system. The following year she gave her first solo *koto* recital; it was to be the last recital she played solely on the thirteen-stringed *koto* (essentially the *gagaku* instrument, but long since modernized with synthetic strings and heavier movable bridges).

Nosaka's path to fame was her choice to participate in the contemporary music scene while remaining faithful to her roots. It was always assumed in the hereditary way of doing things that Keiko Nosaka would eventually take her mother's place as head of their group, the Matsu no Mi Kai of the Ikuta *ryū* (which she did in 2002; she took her mother's artistic name, Soju, with a formal concert in fall 2003). However, in 1965 she joined the then-radical Nihon Ongaku Shudan (Ensemble Nipponia), a group of virtuoso players organized by the composer Minoru Miki (b. 1930) for the purpose of performing contemporary music on traditional instruments (figure 3.6). Feeling musically confined by the constraints of the thirteen-stringed instrument, Nosaka, with Miki's encouragement, caused the creation of a *koto* with first twenty, then

FIGURE 3.6 *Composer Minoru Miki rehearsing a piece for violin, cello, Chinese pipa, and percussion. Tokyo, May 2002.* (Photo by the author.)

twenty-one, now twenty-five strings. Her second solo recital (1969) premiered the new instrument with "Tennyō" (CD track 18), composed by Miki for the occasion.

A new instrument calls for new repertoire, but it was not the first time a need for a new repertoire has been a force in the history of *koto* music. Indeed, expansion of repertoire has contributed greatly to the popularizing of the *koto* through time. As I trace that a bit, note three recurring points: (1) the connection of group identity with repertoire; (2) connections made by *koto*ists with other internal musical spheres; and (3) embracing of the interface with international music.

Tsukushi-goto.   Fleeing to the southern island of Kyushu in the turbulence that established the Kamakura shogunate (1185–1333), many aristocrats brought along instruments of their court culture, the *koto* among them. Its history is a mystery until the sixteenth century, when it resurfaced with a priest-musician, Kenjun (1534?–1623), who had learned *gagaku* compositions at a Buddhist temple and assembled a set of pieces that drew on that music. Called Tsukushi-*goto*, the repertoire was played usually in temples by educated males—Buddhist priests, scholars, and noblemen. Its function was contemplation, not entertainment as *koto* music had been in the Heian court culture. Teaching it to women or to blind male musicians—who were the bearers of more popular culture of the time—was forbidden.

Yatsuhashi Ryū *and "Rokudan."*   Although forbidden, diffusion of the repertoire beyond the Tsukushi group did not take long. Away from Kyushu, in Edo a student of the second head of the group taught a talented blind musician who later became known as Yatsuhashi Kengyō (1624–1715). Yatsuhashi has loomed as an important figure among the composers of traditional *koto* music since; like all others, he was a performer-composer. Notably, he connected the elite *koto* world with the more popular world of *syamisen*. Yatsuhashi Kengyō adopted from *syamisen* modal practice the popular scale that is recognized as distinctively "Japanese" now, with a nucleus of five pitches (with the ascending intervals of whole step, half step, major third, and half-step, as in pitches A B C E F). You can hear that scale on CD track 6, the first section (*dan*) of a piece called "Rokudan" ("Six Sections") that is attributed to Yatsuhashi Kengyō. (The title *Kengyō* indicates a high-ranking musician in the guild established by the Tokugawa government to govern blind musicians.)

Alone among all other music for *koto* until the twentieth century, "Rokudan" and other pieces of the *danmono* (literally "sectional piece") type are entirely for solo *koto*. With "Etenraku," "Rokudan" is among the canon of traditional compositions that every Japanese schoolchild learns about; it is also the piece toward which many young women work in their *koto* lessons, as the goal for sufficient musical achievement for a good marriage. I shall use it below to make several points about how the musical style of traditional *koto* music contrasts with contemporary compositions such as "Tennyō."

Ikuta Kengyō and Yamada Kengyō.   Two particularly important figures followed Yatsuhashi Kengyō in the development of the *koto*. The first was an enterprising *koto*ist, Ikuta Kengyō (1656–1715), who started his own "school" (*ryū*) and who took *koto* closer to *syamisen* music by putting the two instruments together in ensemble. In the Edo area, somewhat later, another prominent *koto* player, Yamada Kengyō (1757–1817), likewise established a *ryū* with distinctive and more narrative compositions.

The *koto* was subservient to the *syamisen* at first, just joining it in accompaniment in *jiuta* vocal pieces (regional songs of the Osaka–Kyoto area). Ikuta *ryū* musicians in the eighteenth and into the nineteenth centuries gradually increased the role of the instruments, thereby expanding the vocal forms to include increasingly longer instrumental interludes. A form called *tegotomono* featured one or more lengthy instrumental sections (*tegoto*). Two-part compositions put the *koto* and *syamisen* in equal prominence. Such pieces written for *koto* were generically called *sōkyoku* to distinguish them from *jiuta* compositions that were composed for *syamisen*.

Michio Miyagi and **Shin Nihon Ongaku.** Further major steps in the popularization of *koto* music were taken by Michio Miyagi (1894–1956), one of the most important *hōgaku* musicians of the twentieth century. Not only did a subgroup of the Ikuta *ryū* form around him, but he also connected with another sphere of traditional music, and became a key player in the interface of traditional music with contemporary Western music.

Miyagi was born in the Meiji period, when the new school music was being widely institutionalized (chapter 1). European music was being taught in the schools in the movement for modernization—a national cultural policy that created a space for an imaginative musician such as Miyagi. Furthermore, as the son of a clerk of a trading company in Kobe, where foreign companies were clustered, he was continually exposed to international culture. When he was blinded by disease during childhood, it was decided that he should enter the music field, which was one of the few occupations available to the blind. From age eight he was apprenticed to traditional musicians to study *koto* and *syamisen*. Family difficulties made a professional of him at age eleven, after only three years of training, for his father, now working in Korea, was seriously injured by burglars. Miyagi had to become an assistant to his teacher in order to support himself and his grandmother in Kobe. At age thirteen, however, he had to leave Kobe for Korea to care for his father and do his best at supporting him and five other family members in the foreign country. Good teachers of the traditional type were not available in Korea at that time, so he could no longer study performance. In Inchon, near Seoul, he began to teach what little he had learned of *koto* and *syamisen* music. To increase his options and the number of students, he taught himself to play *syakuhati*. Growing tired of playing the limited number of pieces he had been privileged to learn in traditional study, Miyagi began composing. Had he been living within the traditional music world in Japan, he would probably not have been permitted to function as a composer until much later in his career.

Miyagi's early exposure to Western music was reinforced in Korea and later. Having befriended amateur *syakuhati* players among the members of a Western military band in Seoul, he heard many band concerts and became familiar with those instruments. He listened avidly to imported phonograph recordings. Encouraged by a friend to go to Tokyo, where both traditional Japanese music and music from European countries flourished, he left Korea as a twenty-one-year old professional musician. After two years of struggling, he gave a recital in 1917 featuring pieces composed during his Korea period. While those pieces seem close to traditional *koto* music, they were sufficiently different to capture the attention of nontraditional enthusiasts; his works were welcomed by those who were in the circle of Western music rather than by those in the *hōgaku* world. Already by 1917 there were two fairly distinct musical worlds in Tokyo.

Encouraged by that success, Miyagi began a period of intensive study of European music theory, composition, violin, and piano, along with general European culture and literature. That led him to create the seventeen-stringed *koto*—a bass *koto* meant initially to function with the thirteen-stringed *koto* like a string bass or cello with the violin (CD track 19).

Miyagi achieved formal affiliation with two of the most significant institutions for music in Japan in the first half of the twentieth century. In 1924 the thirty-year-old artist accepted a proposal from pioneering *syakuhati* master Tozan Nakao to ally himself with the Tozan *ryū*, which had developed into a large, nationwide organization. This alliance helps explain the rapid dissemination of Miyagi's compositions, and it also explains the prominence of the *syakuhati* in many of them.

The next crucial alliance came in 1930 when he was appointed to the faculty of the Tokyo School of Music, which would become Geidai, the historical seat of European musical instruction in Japan. In response to the school's well-trained students and large ensembles (orchestra and chorus), he composed many syncretic pieces, some with chorus and some for large ensembles of Japanese instruments—both startling innovations from the perspective of traditional *koto* music. For *koto* he tried such things as metered pieces, songs with Western-style melodies, use of the instrument as chordal accompaniment to song, and pairing with European instruments. While many of Miyagi's pieces have faded into musical history, his innovations became incorporated into "the tradition," categorized as *Shin Nihon Ongaku*, "New Japanese Music." A portion of one of his most enduring syncretic compositions, "Haru no umi" ("The Ocean in Spring") is reproduced as CD track 20. Conceived originally for *koto* and *syakuhati*, this version is for *koto* and violin to demonstrate how Miyagi bridged the two musical worlds. Miyagi was a gifted musician who seized the moment, changed *koto* music forever, and set the stage for other equally determined and creative musicians such as Keiko Nosaka, Minoru Miki, and Toru Takemitsu.

Traditional Music for Koto.   Here I return to the seventeenth-century piece "Rokudan" to explore some characteristics of traditional *koto* music. The traits noted here apply to that solo instrumental genre (*danmono*) and also to instrumental portions of later pieces composed in traditional style. (I am not speaking here to song portions of *koto* pieces.)

A kind of motion I describe as "flowing ongoingness" gives this music its melodic and rhythmic feel. There is nothing like a tune. Furthermore, although some patterns recur in this music—in "Rokudan" the brief opening motive recurs as a cadential (ending) pattern—thematic motives are not developed.

The melody is intimately linked to the tuning to which the *koto* bridges are set. "Rokudan" is in *hirajoshi* tuning, which consists of five basic pitches on strings 2–6 and higher octaves of those pitches as follows.

2 & 7	octave
3 & 8	octave
4 & 9	octave
5 & 1	unison, 10 is an octave higher
6 & 11	octave
7 & 12	octave
8 & 13	octave

As shown in figure 3.7, additional melodic pitches are gained by pushing down with the left hand to the left side of a movable bridge. By the degree of increased tension, a pitch higher by a half step, a whole step, and even a step and a half can be attained. The left hand is also used for ornamenting the melodic pitches.

ACTIVITY 3.3 *To study* koto *melody, refer to figure 3.8, one* koto *group's notation of the first section of "Rokudan," and the key to reading it in figure 3.7. (Each group has its own notation system, a visible assertion of group identity.)*

- Prepare a sheet of music paper modeled on the notation, but with empty columns and boxes. The first space at the top of column 1 (to the right) contains the title ("Rokudan no shirabe"), and in smaller characters, the name of the tuning (*hirajoshi*). Below that, the small characters say "beginning section," and below that, the string numbers start.

- Translate the Japanese string numbers into Arabic numbers. That is, reproduce the notation, but with Arabic numbers. Copy the other signs as they are, referring to the key to understand them.

- Listen to CD track 6 until you can more or less follow the notation of this, the slowest portion of the piece.

In this *koto* melody, octave patterns are significant, as they add considerable activity and tension to the "flowing ongoingness." Furthermore, analysis of traditional *koto* music has shown me that, beyond octave patterns, melody more or less follows the tuning to which the movable bridges of the *koto* are set.

ACTIVITY 3.4 *Use the transnotation you made for activity 3.3 for this analysis.*

- Bracket to the left all successively plucked strings that outline an octave (or unison in strings 1 and 5). For example, in the sixth box in column 1, you will find a pattern in which strings 3 and 4 are struck in such quick succession as to sound simultaneously, played first with the index finger and then with the middle finger; that is followed in the next count by plucking string 8 with the thumb. Strings 3 and 8 are tuned to an octave, so you should bracket that brief pattern. The

- The notation is vertical: read from the right-most column, from the top down.
- Each box is one count.
- Four counts are grouped by use of double horizontal lines, but you should not expect the first of the four counts to feel stressed in the music.
- The main characters in the boxes indicate the number of the string to be plucked.
- A number written smaller and slightly to the right is of shorter duration.
- Two numbers written side by side are to be played in a single stroke. ⁼⁼
- Repetition is shown by ⟩
- Other symbols:
    - ⊙ Think of the pitch just produced as being prolonged through another beat (although the sound will die away)
    - ○ Silence (i.e., a rest) for a whole count
    - ⚶ Before plucking, push down on the string with the left hand on the far side of the bridge, to raise the pitch by a full step. If small to lower left, push after plucking
    - ⏋ Before plucking, push down on the string with the left hand on the far side of the bridge, to raise the pitch by a half step.
    - ᴇ Grasping the string between the thumb and two fingers, push gently toward the bridge, then release to create a subtle ornament after plucking.
    - 2,3 An arabic numeral indicates the finger number (besides the thumb) used to pluck.
    - △ Suggesting prolonging the previous pitch for half a count

String numbers:

一	二	三	四	五	六	七	八	九	十	斗	為	巾
1	2	3	4	5	6	7	8	9	10	11	12	13

String 13 is the closest to the player, and the highest pitch.

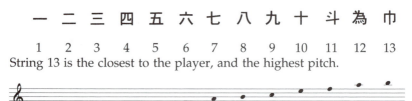

FIGURE 3.7   *Key to reading Miyagi school notation for 13-stringed* koto *(See figure 3.8)*

74

FIGURE 3.8 *First dan of "Rokudan."* *(Reproduced by courtesy of the Miyagi Michio Kinenkan.)*

> percussive striking of strings 2 and 3 together adds vitality to the texture of the melody.
>
> - Bracket to the right side of the numbers all those places where the melody is played on consecutive strings, whether the string numbers are going up or going down. In this way, you will see how the melody follows the tuning.
> - Consider how much (or how little) of *dan* 1 consists of "other" melody.

Rhythmically, the notation gives the visual impression of regular beats. Furthermore, the double lines between sets of four boxes give the impression of a meter—specifically, $\frac{4}{4}$, with its expected stresses on beats 1 and 3. No meter is intended in this traditional music, however, as you can hear on CD track 6. The nonmetric rhythmic flow of traditional *koto* music—a big factor in that "flowing ongoingness"—is probably the one element of the style that is being most affected by Western music enculturation. To my hearing, most *koto* players now unconsciously fall into the trap of stressing first counts in those notated boxes, coming perilously close to turning this into metered music. For that reason, I chose a mid-twentieth-century recording for the CD.

Melody is performed in a straightforward, unemotional way, without exploiting dynamic range or other expressive techniques. In *koto* music that includes song (and most does), the words of the text convey feeling, not the performance of them or the melody to which they are set. On a recording of a whole piece you would hear the speed gradually increase, requiring considerable virtuosity.

Contemporary Composition for Koto.   Unlike the traditional thirteen-stringed instrument, and unlike Miyagi's seventeen-stringed *koto*, Nosaka's twenty-stringed *koto* has always been intended for solo instrumental music. While Nosaka was able to keep its structure and sound close to that of the traditional *koto*, it does offer considerable advantages for *koto*ists who want to play contemporary compositions. Its greater number of strings, for instance, permit a wider pitch range. Composers have experimented widely with tunings, departing from the constraint of orientation to the octave, writing melody as tuneful (or nontuneful) as they wish. The wider body, with its larger resonating chamber, offers composers and players a greater dynamic range, which they usually choose to exploit.

Perhaps most significantly for the gradual popularization of the *koto*, Nosaka has kept the twenty-stringed instrument free of the musical constraint of group musical identity. She has taken the *koto* beyond boundaries into its own cultural space, for any other performers to play and any other composers to explore in the creation of an entirely new repertoire.

> **ACTIVITY 3.5** *Composers since the second half of the twentieth century have been able to choose whether to write music that relates stylistically to traditional* koto *music or not. Review the excerpt from Miyagi's* "Haru no umi" *(CD track 20) and use the portion of* "Tennyō" *on CD track 18 to review this whole section on* koto *music. Try to articulate some similarity or difference you note between them and the* dan *of* "Rokudan" *(CD track 6).*

FROM THEATER TO FILM

Literally as World War II was ending in 1945 with an announcement to the nation by Emperor Hirohito, the filmmaker Akira Kurosawa was engaged in completing *Men Who Step on the Tiger's Tail* (*Tora no o fumu otokotachi*). Through the contemporary medium of a feature film, Kurosawa was connecting a war-torn nation with its history—the second half of the twelfth century—when the country was no longer politically united by the emperor. Competing clans, the Genji and the Heike, struggled for many bloody years for control. In his choice of a story for the film, Kurosawa was drawing on material deeply embedded in Japanese cultural memory: *Heike monogatari* (*Tales of the Heike*), the great prose epic account of those dramatic times, had provided material for martial themes since the thirteenth century. Kurosawa's film is a twentieth-century retelling of a story told and retold as ballad drama, orally and in writing, by wandering minstrels in the medieval period, as theater in the elegant *nō* drama style from the fifteenth century (*Ataka*), as drama in the popular *kabuki* theater (*Kanjinchō*) and more sophisticated *bunraku* puppet theater (*Narihibiku Ataka no Shinseki*) styles since the nineteenth century, and in other forms. The story has moved in and out of popular culture, providing a literally dramatic example of the process of popularization that has characterized Japanese cultural items through time. It also provides exemplary illustration of intertextuality, a theme in this textbook that is the focus of the next chapter.

In *Men Who Step on the Tiger's Tail*, the struggle for power between the Heike and Genji clans has ended with the Minomoto family (Genji clan) victorious. Yoritomo Minamoto emerged as the powerful individual who founds the Kamakura Shogunate (1185–1333). Unfortunately, in 1187 a desperate internecine struggle ensues between Yoritomo and his younger brother Yoshitsune, a lieutenant (*hōgan*) who had stood with him in many battles. Now Yoritomo has turned against his brother. Sorrowfully, Yoshitsune is fleeing from the capital, forced to take a dangerous route over a mountain pass that is guarded by a military barrier on the orders of his brother. Fleeing with the elegant, courtly, but *samurai*-class Yoshitsune is the real hero of the story, Benkei, his loyal retainer-warrior who devises a plan by which they and their small band of men will try to get through the barrier: Yoshitsune will be disguised as a lowly baggage carrier (*gōriki*) and the small band will be disguised as mountain monks (*yamabushi*, real characters of considerable interest in the medieval period). In charge of the barrier is Togashi, a high-ranking officer from that province of Kaga, and his men. What happens there you will discover in the next chapter.

Surely Akira Kurosawa considered the story of unswerving loyalty to be appropriate in 1945, when the seemingly unending war in the Pacific was causing untold suffering for the loyal citizens of Japan. Kurosawa was also a man of the theater, however, who adjusted the play to the times and to the needs of his audience. With the rising comedic actor Enoken in mind, he turned to the *nō* drama version of the play, resuscitated the role of the "real" baggage carrier in Yoshitsune's band of men that the *kabuki* version eliminated, and drew further on *nō* tradition to make the role a comic one (*kyogen*). For music, the composer/arranger Tadashi Hattori reached into *nō*, *kabuki*, *matsuri bayashi*, 1940s-style male choral singing, and also the orchestra, intertextualizing one tradition after another for the purposes of the contemporary, popularized form. I recommend that you watch the film, if possible (see the list of resources at the end of this book).

In this chapter I have illustrated the process of popularization that has characterized the arts in Japan for many centuries, wherein music instruction has been taken beyond classical music, court music and instruments beyond the court, meditation music beyond the temple, folk music into popular concerts, *koto* and its music into fusion with European music, and traditional theater into film. In the next chapter I shall focus on the theme of intertextuality.

CHAPTER 4

Intertextuality in the Theatrical Arts

∞

> *The intertextual effort: "The complex and variegated play of borrowing,*
> *citation, implicit or explicit references . . . and substitutions, which*
> *substantiate the relationships between the texts of a given culture*
> *(and even between texts of different cultures)."*
>
> (De Marinis 1993: 4).

From early instances of recorded poetry to popular music of the present day, creative Japanese, including musicians and other performing artists, have pursued "the intertextual effort" with relish. In this chapter I shall illustrate that effort through the story of Yoshitsune and Benkei, the heroes of the medieval-period *Tales of the Heike*, an epic that has endured with reinterpretation in multiple performance styles. You will see instances of explicit borrowing, as passages of prose and poetry recur in the *nō* play *Ataka*, the *kabuki* play *Kanjinchō*, and the film *Men Who Step on the Tiger's Tail*. You will also see musical material explicitly or implicitly referenced among them. However, the different ways in which the story is reinterpreted are significant as well. I begin with the *nō* drama, because it is the basis for subsequent theatrical versions.

THE *NŌ* DRAMA AND *ATAKA*

The stylistic features of the *nō* drama were set by the early fifteenth century, having been molded by an intertextual effort—ingenious combining and recasting of previously existing dance, music, and theatrical entertainment forms. The history of its development is the history of its patronage and the artistry of individuals—the playwright and theorist Motokiyo Zeami (1363?–1443?) and his playwright father Kan'ami (1333?–1384?), members of a traveling troupe of performers attached to a Buddhist temple in Nara. In 1374 Kan'ami received the signal honor of being invited to perform before the *shōgun*, the young Yoshimitsu Ashikaga (1358–1408), in Kyoto. Motokiyo, then a boy, also appeared onstage. Yoshimitsu instantly fell in love with him and removed him from his father's care. This son of a provincial actor was now the protégé of the most powerful man in Japan, and he received his education from the greatest men of letters of his time. Under those extraordinary circumstances, Zeami's artistry flourished (Tyler 1992: 66).

During the time Yoshimitsu, the third *shōgun* of the Ashikaga Shogunate (1336–1573), was in power Japan experienced a period of peace and stability with a warrior class (*samurai*) fully in charge. One can understand how Zeami, patronized by wealthy, highly educated men steeped in Zen Buddhism (the sect of the *samurai* class), might envisage an aesthetic theory and form that expressed at once elegance and the striving for simplicity that is characteristic of Zen. An intricate fusion of music, dance, mask, costume, and language, the *nō* performing style became specifically associated with that elite level of society.

In *nō* the aesthetic principle of "maximum effect from a minimum of means" can be seen in many ways, including the staging, the plays, the acting and musical forces, movement, and music. Only the costumes (and some masks) defy the principle; displaying the wealth of the social class it was intended to entertain, the costumes of the leading characters are gorgeously embroidered silk, even when representing the character of a monk as in *Ataka* (figure 4.1).

The Staging.   *Nō* was originally presented in small wooden pavilions on temple grounds. Pillars at four corners, which became important reference points for the actors, support the roof. The walkway connecting the pavilion to other temple buildings became a location for dramatic entrances and action; all flooring was highly polished to permit a stylized, sliding style of movement by the actor-dancers. The stage backdrop consisted of a single pine tree painted onto a rear wall. That simple setting has been retained to the present; in modern *nō* theaters, the pavilion and walkway are reconstructed inside a building—a theater inside a theater—and the backdrop remains the single pine, permanently painted onto the back wall. Also, the number of theatrical props is still kept to a minimum. Lighting does not change in the course of a performance.

The Plays and Musical Setting.   For many plays the playwright is known; *Ataka* was fashioned from *Tales of the Heike* by Kojiro Nobumitsu (1435–1516) of the Kanze hereditary lineage of actors. Texts have always

FIGURE 4.1   *Scene from the* nō *play* Ataka (Ha *fifth* dan, *CD track 21*): *Benkei* (shite) *and his men* (tsure) *challenge Togashi* (waki) *and his man* (tsure) *at the barrier. In the rear: pine tree stage backdrop and stage assistants (to the left). Middle: musicians. To the far right: chorus.*   *(Courtesy of the Noh Research Archives, Musashino University.)*

been transmitted in writing (figure 4.2). Nowadays amateurs can be seen studying the small books on the subway, singing to themselves, and aficionados follow the lines as they are delivered in performance.

Over time, plays were classified into types. *Ataka* is a "living-person drama," or "warrior play"; that is, it is based on the story of a real character who was usually a warrior. Plays in that category as a whole are especially dramatic. (The other categories are god, woman, madwoman or miscellaneous, and devil.) Since plays are short, five plays (one in each category) would traditionally be presented in succession, with lighter entertainment (*kyōgen,* miniature comedies) provided at the breaks. As the performance style grew increasingly refined over the course of the centuries, the pace slowed, and a play that would have taken about a half hour to perform now takes about an hour or more. Consequently, if you attend a performance at a *nō* theater at present, you will see fewer plays on a given day.

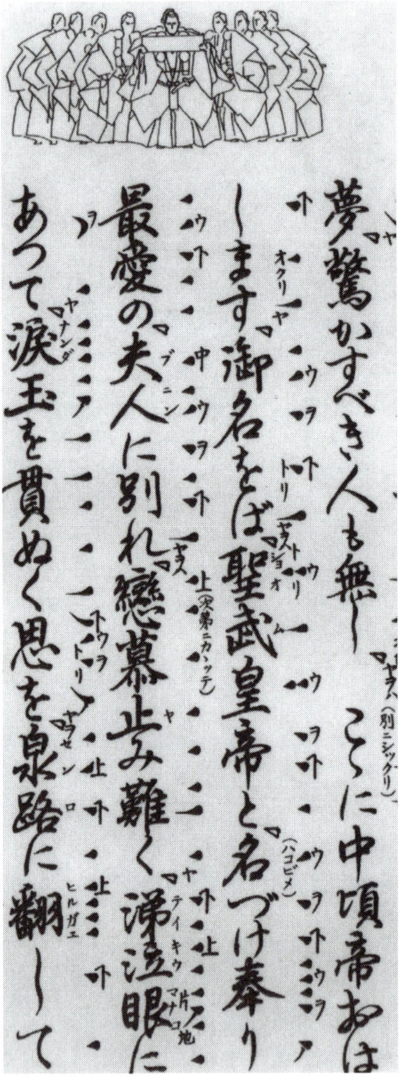

あつて涙玉を貫ぬく思を泉路に翻して

最愛の夫人に別れ戀慕止み難く涕泣眼に

します御名をば聖武皇帝と名づけ奉り

夢鶯かすべき人も無しこゝに中頃帝おは

FIGURE 4.2 *Passages from the Kita ryū libretto of Ataka. The sketch shows Benkei "reading" from the subscription scroll (kanjinchō).*

Structurally, each play is thought of in two ways: in the aesthetic structure of *jo-ha-kyū* that you are familiar with from *gagaku*, and as a series of sections and subsections. The major sections (*dan*, the same word as is used in *koto* music) you can think of as scenes. The beginning, *jo* (labeled *jo no dan*, "a *dan* of *jo*" in figure 4.3), establishes the characters and setting of the play. *Ataka* is shown in figure 4.3 with five *ha dan*, in which the plot is developed. The denouement takes place in a *kyū dan*. Even as you locate them in figure 4.3, remember that it is often a matter of opinion where the *jo-ha-kyū* as well as *dan* begin and end. In the text of *Ataka* that I am referencing, for instance, *jo* consists of Togashi introducing himself, and the allusion to travel of some sort— geographical or psychological; usually thought of as being *jo*-like material, in this version of *Ataka*, it occurs as *ha* first *dan*. For many plays those large divisions are unimportant to the sense and flow of the performance.

What is important for the flow is the performing style of subsections (*shōdan*); scenes usually comprise several subsections. Subsections are distinguished from each other by a mix and match of several traits. The nature of the text is one such trait—whether it is prose, free verse, or poetry that is strictly defined by syllable counts. The style in which the text is rendered is another trait, as is the use of the instruments in the *nō* ensemble, and others. Moving in and out of the various subsectional formats creates a kind of dramatic action. In figure 4.4 (p. 104) you will find subsections that occur in the CD examples listed in alphabetical order. You can begin to sense the flow among them by locating them in figure 4.3, printed in italic lettering.

ACTIVITY 4.1 *A transliteration and translation of parts of Ataka are given in figure 4.3 as a study text. Locate in it the references to the CD tracks, as you have already located the major sections (dans) and subsections (shōdan). For reference, flag the passages I address below in this Activity.*

- Read the translation for a sense of the whole play.
- The *mondō* subsection in *Ha* Fifth *dan* is the first passage on the CD (track 21). Beginning with it, and proceeding to other recorded passages, listen for the purpose of following the text

(Activity 4.1 continues on pp. 104–5.)

Jo no dan Togashi introduces himself and gives orders to his guards to watch out for *yamabushi* (mountain monks).

Chorus

Ha first dan begins with *hayashi* entry music (not on CD)

(Shidai: au tsuyogin)	
Tabi o koromo wa	Dressed in the traveling robes of monks
Suzukake no,	
Tabi no koromo wa	Dressed in the traveling robes of monks
Suzukake no	
Tsuyukeki sode ya	Sweeping the dew,
Shioruran.	our sleeves are drenched.

(Sashi) Benkei and his men review their journey, explain that their Lord (Benkei) is disguised as chief among the monks, they are setting out again.

Benkei and his men

(Ageuta: au, tsuyogin)	
Toki shimo koro wa	It is the tenth day
Kisaragi no,	of the second month,
Toki shimo koro wa	It is the tenth day
Kisaragi no,	of the second month,
Kisaragi no	From Miyako
Tōka no yo	drenched in moonlight,
Tsuki no Miyako o	from the moon-bright capital
Tachi idete,	we set forth on our way.
"Kore ya kono	"Oh, there lies the Hill of Meeting
Yuku mo kaeru mo	where travelers who come and go,
wakarete wa,	where travelers who come and go,
Yuku mo kaeru mo	both friends and strangers,
Wakarete wa,	though once parted, shall ever meet again."
Shiru mo shiranu mo."	But oh! The mist conceals
Osaka no	the lovely hill from sight;
Yama kakusu	
"Kasumi zo haru wa	"How hateful is the mist in spring!"
Urameshiki."	

(Sageuta: au tsuyogin)	
Namiji haruka ni	Sailing on the pathways of the waves,
Yuku fune no,	
Namiji haruka ni	Sailing on the pathways of the waves,

FIGURE 4.3   *The nō play Ataka. The English translation is mainly based on that in* Japanese Noh Drama, *vol. 3 (Tokyo: Nippon Gakujutsu Shinkokai, 1953), 149–72. Revisions and changes to match the Kita ryū version were made by Janice Kande.*

(continued)

Part 1 Togashi introduces himself and gives orders to his guards to watch out for *yamabushi*.

Part 2 begins with *nō hayashi* entry music (CD track 27)

Singers (at 0:39)

Tabi no koromo wa	Dressed in the traveling robes of monks
Suzukake no,	
Tabi no koromo wa	Dressed in the traveling robes of monks
Suzukake no	
Tsuyukeki sode ya	Sweeping the dew,
Shioruran.	our sleeves are drenched.

(Sashi of nō skipped in kabuki)

Benkei and his men

Toki shimo koro wa	It is the tenth day
Kisaragi no,	of the second month,

Kisaragi no	From Miyako
Tōka no yo	drenched in moonlight,
Tsuki no Miyako o	from the moon-bright capital
Tachi idete	we set forth on our way.
"Kore ya kono	"Oh, there lies the Hill of Meeting
Yuku mo kaeru mo	where travelers who come and go,
wakarete wa,	
	both friends and strangers,
	though once parted, shall ever meet again."
Shiru mo shiranu mo."	But oh! The mist conceals
Osaka no	the lovely hill from sight;
Yama kakusu	
"Kasumi zo haru wa	"How hateful is the mist in spring!"
Urameshiki."	

Namiji haruka ni	Sailing on the pathways of the waves,
Yuku fune no,	
Namiji haruka ni	Sailing on the pathways of the waves,

FIGURE 4.11 *The* kabuki *play* Kanjinchō. *English translation is based mainly on* Ataka, *in* Japanese Noh Drama, *vol. 3 (Tokyo: Nippon Gakujutsu Shinkokai, 1953), 149–72, and on James R. Brandon and Tamako Niwa, adapt.,* Kanjin-cho, *in* Kabuki Plays "Kanjincho" "The Zen Substitute" *(New York: Samuel French, 1966), 1–48. Revisions and adjustments for the performed version were made by Janice Kande.*

(continued)

Yuku fune no
Kaizu no ura ni   we reach the Kaizu shore.
tsukinikeri.

Exchange between Benkei and his men, informing us that they have arrived at the port of Ataka.

Ha second *dan*
Conversation between Benkei and his Lord, Yoshitsune (sometimes Y hereafter), then between Benkei and his men. One retainer responds for the men. Benkei explains his plan to Y, who agrees to be disguised as a porter. Benkei relieves their servant (a real baggage carrier, *gōriki*) of his pack and sends him to the barrier to scout the situation. The *gōriki* speaks what he observes—the heads of decapitated *yamabushi*—and returns to report to Benkei.

In an exchange of verses, Benkei and his men dress Yoshitsune as a porter, hiding his face under a big hat, instructing him how to walk pitifully under his burden. Then, telling Y to walk at the rear, they set off to the barrier.

Ha third *dan*   At the barrier
The swordbearer of Togashi (chief of the barrier guards) informs Togashi that *yamabushi* are approaching. Togashi responds, and Benkei tells him that they are monks traveling to raise funds for the rebuilding of the Tōdaiji temple at Nara. Togashi explains why they cannot pass—the Yoritomo and Yoshitsune dispute. "You are ordered to stop false *yamabushi*, but surely not true ones," answers Benkei. Yes, is the answer, even if the *hōgan* (Y) is not among them. Benkei tells his men to prepare for their fate.

The text is almost the same in *nō* and *kabuki*, with drums punctuating the dialogue in heightened speech.

Benkei
Ide ide saigo no   Come, let us begin our final offices.
tsutome wo nasan.
Sore yamabushi to   According to the faith of En no Ubasoku,
ippa, En no Ubasoku   the saint, they follow.
no byōgi wo uke.

FIGURE 4.3 *Continued.*

(continued)

Yuku fune no	
Kaizu no ura ni	we reach the Kaizu shore.
tsukinikeri.	

Part 3

Conversation follows between Benkei and his lord, Yoshitsune, then between Benkei and his men, Benkei explains to Y his plan to disguise him as a baggage carrier and Y agrees. The men are instructed accordingly and each responds with a line; sharing the dialogue in that manner is *kabuki*-like where stage action is emphasized. This dialogue is punctuated by strokes on the *ō-tsuzumi* and *ko-tsuzumi*.

The chorus of *nagauta* singers accompanies their proceeding to near the barrier gate.

Part 4 At the barrier

Benkei calls to a barrier guard, saying they are *yamabushi* who wish to pass. Togashi responds, and Benkei tells him that they are monks traveling to raise funds for the rebuilding of the Tōdaiji temple at Nara. Togashi explains why they cannot pass—the Yoritomo and Yoshitsune dispute. "You are ordered to stop false *yamabushi*, but surely not true ones," answers Benkei. "Yes," is the response, "even if the *hōgan* (Y) is not among them." Benkei tells his men to prepare for their fate.

The text is almost the same in *nō* and *kabuki*, with drums punctuating the dialogue in heightened speech. Again, however, the guards are given individual lines.

Part 5 (CD track 26 starts at *)

These lines extracted from the *nō* exchange create a new unit:

Benkei

Ide ide saigo no	Come, let us begin our final offices.
tsutome wo nasan.	
Sore yamabushi to	According to the faith of En no Ubasoku,
ippa, En no Ubasoku	the saint they follow,
no byōgi wo uke,	
Sokushin sokubutsu	Whoever here kills a *yamabushi*,

FIGURE 4.11 *Continued.*

(continued)

An exchange between Benkei and his men ensues, laden with Buddhist formulas and symbolism, as they "do their final offices."

Chorus

(awazu, tsuyogin)	
Onnabira	Oh! Earth, Water, Fire,
unken to	Wind, and Air! They chant,
juzu sarasara to	rubbing hard the rosaries
oshimomeba.	raucously aloud.

Ha fourth *dan*

In the next, most-famous scene, Togashi takes up with Benkei his project of raising funds for the rebuilding of the Tōdaiji temple at Nara, saying that Benkei must have a subscription book. He asks Benkei to read from it. Benkei has no such document, but ostentatiously takes an empty scroll from the baggage and pretends to read from it. Togashi attempts twice to see the scroll, but Benkei moves just so he cannot.

    The text is almost the same in *nō* and *kabuki*, up to the point recorded on CD track 26 of the *kabuki*.

FIGURE 4.3   *Continued.*

(continued)

no yamabushi wo,	
Koko nite uchitodome	whose bodies are one and the same with
tawaman ikoto,	Buddha,
Myōō no shoran	Shall be witnessed by Myōō;
hakarigatō,	
Yuya Gongen no	and incur the divine punishment of Yuya
onbatsu atarankoto,	Gongen instantly, verily without doubt.
Tachidokoro ni oite	
utagai bekarazu.	

Singers (for all of Benkei's men)

*Onnabira	Oh! Earth, Water, Fire,
unken to	Wind, and Air! They chant,
juzu sarasara to	rubbing hard the rosaries
oshimonari.	raucously aloud.

Part 6 (CD track 26 at 0:17)

Togashi

Chikagoro shūshō no	This is praiseworthy. You spoke just
onkakugo, osaki ni	now of raising funds for the rebuilding
uketamawari sōraeba,	of the Todaiji temple at Nara, and
Nanto Todaiji no kanjin	doubtless you must be furnished with a
to ōse ari shika, kanjinchō	subscription book.
goshoji naki koto wa	
yomo arumaji.	
Kanjinchō asobasare	Pray, read it.
sōrae. Kore nite chōmon	I will listen to you here.
tsukamatsuru.	

Benkei

Nanto kanjinchō wo yome	What? Read from a subscription
to ōsezōrō wa na.	book, do you say?

Togashi

Ika ni mo.	That is what I said.

Benkei

Mu, kokoroete sōrō.	Very well.

Singer

Moto yori kanjinchō no	Such a book he never had!
araba koso. Oi no uchi	Out of the pack he takes a
yori ōrai no makimono	scroll
ichikan tori idashi,	

FIGURE 4.11 *Continued.*

(continued)

Immediately after the reading, the *dan* ends with this (not on the CD):

Togashi

(Au, tsuyogin)
Seki no hitobito   The terror-stricken guards
kimo o keshi

Chorus
osore o nashite   in awe and trembling
tōshikeri,   let them pass,
osore o nashite   in awe and trembling
tōshikeri.   let them pass.

Ha **fifth** *dan*

Benkei, Y, and their retainers start to leave the barrier. Togashi's sword-bearer, however, has recognized Yoshitsune and gives a warning. Togashi order him to halt. Benkei's retainers, ready to rush forward, exclaim "Here we all sink or swim. All together return to the barrier." Benkei quietly orders the men to be careful and, "noticing" that the porter is not proceeding through the barrier, orders him to pass through. But Togashi explains that he has ordered him to stop. "Why?" asks Benkei, and Togashi responds, "There are those who say he looks like the man we seek."

FIGURE 4.3 *Continued.*

(continued)

kanjinchō to nazuketsutsu	and calling it the subscription
takaraka ni koso yomiage	book, loudly he reads.
kere.	

Benkei (at 2:07)

Sore tsuratsura	As I ponder deeply,
Omon mireba, daionkyōshū	Ever since the Founder of the Law,
no aki no tsuki wa,	like the autumn moon
nehan no kumo ni kakure	wrapped in clouds,
Shoji jōya no nagaki yume	entered the heaven of Nirvana,
odorokasu beki hito	none roused the sleeping world
mo nashi.	from the long dream of life and death,
Koko ni nakagoro no	until there rose an Emperor . . .
Mikado owashimasu . . .	

Part 7 Dissatisfied with the reading, Togashi engages Benkei in a lengthy dialogue, questioning him closely about details of significance to the *yamabushi* Buddhist sect. There is no musical support until one choral line sums up the effect of Benkei's answers: "The barrier warden seems impressed" is sung with *syamisen* accompaniment.

Part 8 Finally Togashi seems convinced and tells them that they may go. Then, in an elaborately staged scene, Togashi has his men bring gifts, his contribution to the project. Benkei thanks him but asks that they keep most of the gifts for them to collect when they return. Benkei then tells his men to hurry and pass through the barrier. The scene ends with:

Singers

Kowa ureshii ya to	Rejoicing within,
yamabushi mo, shizu	the *yamabushi* quietly rise
jizu tatte ayumarekere.	and move away.

Part 9
Benkei, Yoshitsune, and their retainers start to leave the barrier. Togashi's swordbearer, however, has recognized Yoshitsune and gives a warning. Togashi tells the porter (Yoshitsune) to stop, and Benkei quietly orders the men to be careful so they all turn back. "Noticing" that the porter is not proceeding through the barrier, Benkei orders him to pass through. But Togashi explains that he has ordered him to stop. "Why?" asks Benkei, and Togashi responds, "There are those who say he looks like the man we seek."

FIGURE 4.11 *Continued.*

(continued)

Benkei (to the disguised Yoshitsune) (CD track 21)

(mondō: kotoba)

Hōgan-donno ni
Ni mōshitaru gōriki-
me wa ichigo no
omoide na. Haratachi
ya hitakaku wa Noto
no Kuni made
sasōzuru to omoishi
ni wazuka no oi
ōte ato ni
sagareba koso
*hito mo ayashimure.
Sōjite kono hodo

To look like Lord Hōgan will be the memory of a lifetime for this stupid fellow! How angry I am. While the sun was still high, I thought we could stretch our legs and get on to Noto. But here you drag along behind us, though you carry such a light pack. That's why people suspect you.

Lately, I've become

nikushi nikushi to
omoishi ni, idemono
misete kuren tote
kongōzue ottote
sanzan ni chōchakusu.

more and more disgusted with you. I must teach you a lesson.

Snatching up the diamond staff, I beat him repeatedly, shouting,

Tōre to koso.

"Pass on!"

Togashi

Nani to chinji
tamō tomo tōshi mōsu
majiku sōro.

No matter what you may say, I say I will allow not a single one of you to pass.

Benkei

Gōriki o tome oi ni
me o kaketamo wa
tōjin zō na.

Are you stopping the porter because you want to steal something from him?

FIGURE 4.3 *Continued.*

(continued)

Benkei (to the disguised Yoshitsune) (CD track 25 at *)

Hōgan-donno ni
nitaru gōriki-
me wa ichigo no
omoide na. Haratachi
ya hitakaku wa Noto
no Kuni made
kosō zurō to omoirui
ni wazuka no oi
hitotsu se ōte ato ni
sagareba koso,
*hito ni ayashimure.

To look like Lord Hōgan will be the memory
of a lifetime for this stupid fellow! How angry
I am. While the sun was still high, I thought
we could stretch our legs and get on to Noto.
But here you drag along behind us, though
you carry such a light pack. That's
why people suspect you.

Sōjite kono hodo yori,
yaya mo sureba,
Hōgandono yo to
Ayashimerararu wa,
Onore ga waza no
Tsutanaki yue nari.

If people begin suspecting you of being the
Hōgan on the slightest provocation, you'll be
the cause of the failure of our mission.

Omoeba, nikushi,
nikushi, nikushi,
ide monomisen.

The more I think of it, you are hateful!
Hateful! Hateful!
I will teach you!

Singers

Kongōzue ottote
sanzan ni
chōchakusu.

And snatching Hōgan's staff, he
beats him heavily

Benkei

Tōre.

"Pass through, I say!"

Singers

Tōre to koso wa
nonoshirinu.

He berates him soundly, ordering him
to pass.

Togashi

Iya, ika yō ni
chinzutomo, tōsu koto,

No matter what you may say, he shall not

Guards

makari naranu.

pass through.

Benkei

Yaa, oi ni me wo
kaketamō wa
Tōjin zō na.
Kore

Why cast your suspicious eyes on the pack?
You must be thieves!

Here! Here!

FIGURE 4.11   Continued.

(continued)

Chorus (at 0:58)

(Ageuta: au, tsuyogin)	
Katagata wa	Oh, all you guardsmen,
nani yue ni,	what are the reasons,
Katagata wa	Oh, all you guardsmen
nani yue ni,	what are the reasons
kahodo iyashiki	that you draw the swords and blades
gōriki ni	against so lowly
tachi katana	and all too humble
nukitamō wa	a baggage carrier,
medaregao no	in this unmanly way
furumai wa	to act the bully?
Okubyō no	Have you now become
Itari ka to	such utter cowards?
Jūichinin no	Speaking thus, the mountain monks
yamabushi wa	one and ten in all,
uchi katana	start to draw halfway
nukikakete	their swords all ready
isami	and against
kakareru	this heroic
arisama wa	move to face the foe,
ikanaru tenma	all devil-fiends whatever
kijin mo	and demons all,
osoretsubyō zo	horror-struck and filled with awe,
mietaru.	would surrender!

In four further lines spoken without drama, Togashi says he has made a mistake and a guard tells them to pass through.

Ha sixth *dan*

Having passed safely through the barrier, the group stops to rest, and Benkei apologizes humbly to Yoshitsune, who responds.

Yoshitsune (CD track 3)

(Kotoba)	
Ika ni Benkei,	Listen, Benkei, the ready wit you showed just
sate mo tadaima	now could never have been an act sprung
no kitten sara ni	from an ordinary man.

FIGURE 4.3 *Continued.*

(continued)

Singers

Katagata wa	Oh, all you guardsmen,
nani yue ni,	what are the reasons
kahodo iyashiki	that you draw the swords and blades
gōriki ni	against so lowly
tachi katana	and all too humble
nukitamō wa	a baggage carrier,
medaregao no	in this unmanly way
furumai wa	to act the bully?
Okubyō no	Have you now become
Itari ka to	such utter cowards?
Jūichinin no	Speaking thus, the mountain monks
yamabushi wa	one and ten in all,
uchi katana	start to draw halfway
nukikakete	their swords all ready
isami	and against
kakareru	this heroic
arisama wa	move to face the foe,
ikanaru tenma	all devil-fiends whatever
kijin mo	and demons all,
osoretsubyō zo	horror-struck and filled with awe,
mie ni keru.	would surrender!

In dialogue, Benkei tells Togashi that if he thinks the *gōriki* is Yoshi-tsune, then he should hold him with the gifts until they return. He also offers to kill Y. So impressed is Togashi with that, and with Benkei's having sacrificed his own honor by beating his lord, that he decides to let them pass—despite knowing that "the porter" is Yoshitsune and that letting him go means his own disgrace. *Syamisen* and *tsuzumi* accompany elegant stage movement.

Part 10
Whereas in the nō Benkei apologizes to Yoshitsune in a reflective moment of relief, in the *kabuki* version a few phrases from Benkei's apology are incorporated into Yoshitsune's words of forgiveness. He declares Benkei's plan the divine protection of their patron deity, Hachiman, the god of war. Each of the four retainers expresses a reaction, ending with Retainer 1 "We were" and all four retainers "truly amazed!"

FIGURE 4.11 *Continued.*

(continued)

bonryo yori nasu
waza ni arazu.
Tada ten no on-kago   Think of it only as a
to koso omoyeru.   grace from heaven.
(Fushi)
Seki no monodomo   When the barrier guardsmen cast
ware o ayashime,   suspicious eyes upon me,
shōgai kagiri   and this life of mine, I thought,
naritsuru tokoro ni,   had come then to its final hour,
tokaku no zehi oba   decisively, with no questions
mondawazushite   of the right or wrong of it,
tada makoto no   taking me in my guise
genin no gotokku,   of a lowly serving man,
sanzan ni utte   you hit and beat me thoroughly,
ware o tasukuru.   and rescued me from peril.
★Kore Benkei ga   Could this not have been perhaps
Hakarigoto ni arazu   a plan not made by Benkei
Hachiman no   but a way revealed
                              Chorus

(Sageuta: au, yowagin) (at 0:14)
go-takusen ka to   by the mighty God of War?
omoyeba   A miracle!
Katajikenaku zo   When I think of this I feel
oboyuru   deep gratitude.

(Kuri: awazu, yowagin) (at 0:43)
Sore yo wa masse ni   Say that this world of ours has now
oyobu to iedomo   entered the later stage of time,
nichi gata wa imada   still the sun and the moon on high
chi ni ochitamawazu.   have not yet fallen on this earth.

Tatoi ikanaru   Say whatever may be said,
hōben naritomo   for my improvisation,
masashiki shukun o   still, with a staff I struck my lord,
utsu tsuye no   our rightful master.
Tenban ni   Is it not then true
ataranu koto ya   that the judgment of Heaven
arubeki.   must fall on me?

FIGURE 4.3 *Continued.*

(continued)

CD track 15 records Benkei voicing his feelings, with *syamisen* support.

Benkei

Sore yo wa masse ni	Say that this world of ours has now
oyobu to iedomo	entered the later stage of time,
nichi getsu wa imada	still the sun and the moon on high
chi ni ochitamawazu	have not yet fallen on this earth.
gokōurn.	Fate has been kind to Yoshitsune also.
Arigatashi,	How grateful we all are.
*(CD cuts to * below)*	
arigatashi.	
Keiryaku to mōshi-	You speak of strategy, but the fact is that I
nagara, masashiki	struck my own dear Lord. The heavenly
shukun wo chōchaku,	reprisals are frightening to contemplate.
tembatsu sora osoro-	These two arms which can lift a thousand kin
shiku, senkin wo	are as though benumbed.

FIGURE 4.11 *Continued.*

(continued)

Yoshitsune

(Sashi: awazu, yowagin) (at 2:07)

Geni ya genzai no	We see effect that manifests
ka o mite kako	in the present, people say,
mirai o shiru to	so we understand the past
iu koto	and the future,

Chorus

ima ni shirarete	as now I do, from sorrows
mi no ue ni	suffered in my flesh
uki toshi tsuki no	from months and years of hardship
Kisaragi ya	coming to this end
shimo no tōka no	of the frosty second month;
kyō no nan o	that we survived somehow
nogaretsuru koso	the dread dangers of this day
fushigi nare.	is a miracle!

Yoshitsune (at 3:11)

Tada sanagara ni	Overwhelmed, the chosen band
jiyuyonin	of ten men and more

Chorus

Yume no sametaru	are held by the sensation
kokochi shite	of a dreamer roused,
tagai ni omote o	and not yet wakened from his dream.
awasetsutsu	Staring numb and blank
naku bakari naru	from one face to another
arisama kana.	they cry and weep aloud.

This section continues, with a chorus lament for Yoshitsune's fate and for a wretched world.

Kyû dan

The *dan* begins with Togashi deciding to redeem his rudeness to Benkei by offering it and orders his swordbearer to catch up with them. The swordbearer intersects with the real baggage carrier, who carries the message to Benkei. Benkei agrees to drink with Togashi.

Benkei (CD track 22)

(kotoba, speaking to himself)

Geni geni kore mo	Indeed, I know the real reason for this.
kokoroetari. Hito no	With a cup of kindness, he would make us
nasake no sakazuki ni	feel afloat and seize our hearts.

FIGURE 4.3 *Continued.*

(continued)

aguru soregashi, ude	
mo shibiruru gotoku	
oboe sōrō.	
★Ara mottai na ya,	How wrong I have been!
mottai na ya.	How wrong!

	Singer
Tsui ni nakanu	How noble, now, even Benkei
Benkei mo,	
Ikii no namida zo	who has never given way before
reshhō naru.	finally shed the tears of a lifetime.
Hōgan-dono te wo	The Hôgan then took his hand.
tori tamai.	

Part 10 continues with Yoshitsune and Benkei lamenting Y's fate. The singers continue in that mood, with *hayashi* and *syamisen* support. Finally, their retainers urge them, "Quickly now, my Lord, let us withdraw." The chorus narrates: "Pulling on each others' sleeves, they seem anxious to be on their way."

Part 11
Togashi catches up with the party of monks and invites Benkei to drink *sake* with him. Benkei: "My kind Lord, I shall drink with you, with pleasure."

Part 12
The drinking scene ensues. When the two men are thoroughly in their cups, Togashi suggests that Benkei dance.

	Singers (CD track 28)
Geni geni kore mo	Indeed, I know the real reason for this.
kokoroetari. Hito no	When one sips from the cup of another's
nasake no sakazuki ni	compassion, one grows attached to that

FIGURE 4.11 *Continued.*

(continued)

ukete kokoro o toran *to ya. Kore ni tsukite* *mo hitobito ni.*	So regarding this, now more than ever

(Fushi: tsuyogin) *(0:27)*
kokoro na kure so *Kurehatori.*	do not give your hearts away.

Chorus *(0:39)*

(Au, tsuyogin)
ayashimeraru na	Do not let this novelty
menmen to	betray anyone.
Benkei ni	Carefully cautioned thus
isamerarete	by Benkei,
kono yamakage no	in this mountain shade that serves
hitoyadori ni	as their makeshift lodging,
sarari to	arrayed they sit,
matoi shite	by the mountain trail
tokoro mo	this place lies too.
yamaji no	So let this sake
Kiku no sake o	be chrysanthemum wine,
nomō yo.	let us drink it.

Benkei *(at 1:33)*

Omoshiro ya	What a delight it is
yamamizu ni	on the mountain stream,

Chorus

Omoshiro ya	What a delight it is
yamamizu ni	on the mountain stream,
sakazuki o	sake cups are set
ukamete wa	afloating, drifting
riyū ni hikaruru	down the water's rippling flow
kyokusui no	to the crescent bend
te mazu saegirua *sode furete.*	the cups are taken, the wine is drunk.
Iza ya mai o	Let us dance a measure
Maō yo.	with waving rustling sleeves.

Moto yori	Originally
Benkei wa	Benkei served
Santō	the Three Pagodas
no yūsō,	as a young page
mai ennen no toki	dancing at the Ennen Dance.
no waka,	to the timely song.

FIGURE 4.3 *Continued.*

(continued)

ukete kokoro o	person.
todomu to ka ya.	
Ima wa mukashi	And now for tales of the past . . .
no katarigusa,	
ara hazukashi no	What embarrassment my heart once met.
waga kokoro, ichido	once met a woman and confusion.
mamieshi onna sae,	Along the road of confusion,
mayoi no michi no	this barrier once was crossed.
seki koete,	Being crossed, yet another now with
ima mata	difficulty passed.
koko ni koekaneru	
Hitome no seki no	To pass the barrier of people's eyes is
yaruse naya,	difficult to bear.
Aasatorarenukoso	Aah, it is a transient world in which we never
ukiyo nare.	know enlightenment.

Part 12

Omoshiro ya	What a delight it is
yamamizu ni	on the mountain stream,
Omoshiro ya	What a delight it is
yamamizu ni	on the mountain stream,
sakazuki o	sake cups are set
ukamete wa	afloating, drifting
riyū ni hikaruru	down the water's rippling flow
kyokusui no	to the crescent bend
te mazu saegiru	the cups are taken, the wine is drunk.
sode furete.	
Iza ya mai o	Let us dance a measure
Maō yo.	with waving rustling sleeves.

On CD track 29 you will hear a brief version of the *nō Ataka no mai,* then I cut to the following.

FIGURE 4.11   *Continued.*

(continued)

Kore naru	Oh, over here
yamamizu no	the mountain water
ochite iwao ni	falling on the rocks below
hibiku koso	echoes back the line:
"Naru wa taki no	"The booming of the waterfall . . ."
mizu . . ."	

Benkei dances the *Ataka no mai* (except for beginning and end, extracted for CD track 23)

Benkei (CD track 22 at 4:03)

(awazu, tsuyogin)	
"Naru wa taki no	"The booming of the waterfall . . ."
mizu . . ."	

Chorus

(Noriji: ōnori, tsuyogin)	
hi wa terutomo	though the sun burns brightly
tayezu tōtari,	still the booming sounds below,
tayezu tōtari.	still the booming sounds below.
Toku toku tate ya	Quickly, quickly let us go.
tatsukayumi no	Like the bow you hold,
kokoro yurusuna	don't relax your heartstring now;
sekimori no hitobito	listen, guardsmen of the barrier,
itoma mōshite	we must say our parting words,
saraba yo tote.	and bid you all farewell.
Oi o ottori	Lifting up the packs
kata ni uchikake.	they pack them on their shoulders.
Tora no o o fumi	Stepping on the tiger's tail
dokuja no kuchi o	they all feel as though they go
nogaretaru kokochi	escaping from the serpent's poison
shite.	jaws.
Mutsu no Kuni e zo	And to the land of Mutsu
kudarikeru.	they go on their way.

FIGURE 4.3 *Continued.*

Singers (at 1:11)

Kore naru	Oh, over here
yamamizu no	the mountain water
ochite iwao ni	falling on the rocks below
hibiku koso	echoes back the line:
"Naru wa taki no	"The booming of the waterfall . . ."
mizu . . ."	

"Naru wa taki no	"The booming of the waterfall . . ."
mizu . . ."	

(chirashi)

"Naru wa taki no	"The booming of the waterfall . . ."
mizu . . ."	

hi wa terutomo	though the sun burns brightly
tayezu tōtari,	still the booming sounds below,
tayezu tōtari.	still the booming sounds below.
Toku toku tate ya	Quickly, quickly let us go.
tatsukayumi no	Like the bow you hold,
kokoro yurusuna	don't relax your hearstring now;
sekimori no hitobito	listen, guardsmen of the barrier,
itoma mōshite	we must say our parting words,
saraba yo tote.	and bid you all farewell.
Oi o ottori	Lifting up the packs
kata ni uchikake.	they pack them on their shoulders.
Tora no o o fumi	Stepping on the tiger's tail
dokuja no kuchi o	they all feel as though they go
nogaretaru kokochi	escaping from the serpent's poison
shite.	jaws.

(danigire)

Mutsu no kuni e zo	And to the land of Mutsu
kudarikeru.	they go on their way.

FIGURE 4.11 *Continued.*

Ageuta High pitched song (*uta*), usually about ten lines with repetition of first and last lines. In this *ageuta* there are eleven lines (each formatted as two lines in figure 4.3); the first line is repeated, but not the last. Such textual flexibility in the *shōdan* is typical of *nō*. Congruent rhythm.

Ataka no mai A version peculiar to this play of *otoko no mai*, a fairly fast, energetic, masculine dance that emphasizes the beat. Broad movements with angled stance and sharp placement.

Fushi Melody, unaccompanied or accompanied. Sometimes, transition to *yowagin*.

Kotoba Vocal style of stylized speech, usually without drums.

Kuri Ornate song: *yowagin* in high register. Noncongruent rhythm. Flute at beginning and end. Cadence: low-pitched extension of last syllable for eight pulses, wavering flute pattern, cadence pattern on drums.

Mondō Dialogue, in stylized speech, without accompaniment.

Noriji Narrative poetry, *tsuyogin* in high range. Song matched to drums in one-syllable-to-one-beat system. Drums play short, cyclical patterns. (See *Kanjinchō chirashi*.)

Sageuta "Low pitched song," but begins in middle register, shifting back and forth to low, ending low. Verse mostly lines of seven plus five syllables; here, seven plus four. Congruent rhythm in "standard rhythm." Flute in last line in free rhythm.

Sashi Recitative in *yowagin*. Lines usually seven plus five syllables (with variations), but rhythm unmatched to drums.

Shidai Entrance music and opening song.

FIGURE 4.4 Nō *drama subsections* (shōdan)

Activity 4.1 (*continued*)

transliteration. The text is archaic Japanese, and pronunciation of it as performed is a challenge to follow sometimes. If you have difficulty, refer to the pronunciation guide in figure 4.5.

• Note that CD track 21 begins with a prose text.

1. The Japanese language is syllabic. A syllable usually consists of a consonant plus vowel, or a vowel alone, or a nasal (*m* or *n*).
2. Two consecutive vowels are separate syllables. In *shioruran*, for instance, *shio-* is two syllables: *shi* + *o*. *Shioruran* is thus five syllables: *shi* + *o* + *ru* + *ra* + *n*.
3. Sometimes the second of two vowels together is introduced with a *y*, as in *kokoroe* becoming *kokoroye*.
4. Often the vowel *a* is pronounced more like *o*.
5. The consonant *g* is often swallowed.
6. Sometimes syllables are elided, two syllables sounding like one. Just keep listening past such elisions.
7. Sometimes a preposition (*no*, meaning "of") or a grammatical marker (*wo* or *o*, marking the object of a verb) is swallowed.

FIGURE 4.5   *Guide to pronunciation of the* Ataka *text*

- Listen for the shift to poetry at 0:58 ("Katagata wa") in which most (but not all) of the lines are five or seven syllables. A vowel with macron counts as two syllables.
- On CD track 3 (at 2:07) Yoshitsune's short comment beginning "Geni ya genzai no" is in free verse, with lines of seven, six, seven, and four syllables. The chorus that follows immediately from "Ima ni shirarete" is in strict verse, with lines alternating seven and five syllables.

In the *nō* performing style, text is rendered in one of two ways: as heightened speech (*kotoba*), or set to melody (*fushi*) in one of two styles.

- *Yowagin* (or *wagin*, "soft singing") is truly melodic singing in which there are three main pitch areas: low, middle, and high, with the melody emphasizing one area or traveling among them. Between the central tone in each area is an interval of a fourth, that is, between low and middle, and between middle and high. You can also hear pitches above or below each central tone, but they clearly orient to a central tone. "Pitches" are set by the actors or by the chorus leader, changing at their will. It is the pitch level or area that is important, not a specific pitch frequency.

• *Tsuyogin* ("strong singing") is a dynamic, forceful singing mode that is more like chant than singing. There is much less sense of real pitch areas. Starting on a fairly low pitch, the pitch may rise gradually. This style is derived from Buddhist chant.

ACTIVITY 4.2   *Listen without following the text to hear the differences among* kotoba, yowagin, *and* tsuyogin. Ha *sixth* dan *has begun with* kotoba; *CD track 3, however, begins in the next subsection in* fushi *(at "Kore"), as a kind of transition to truly melodic* yowagin *singing at 0:14. On CD track 22* Benkei *begins speaking to himself in* kotoba *style, then shifts subtly into* fushi tsuyogin *at 0:27; at 0:39 the chorus shifts the texture clearly to* tsuyogin.

Next, study the text translation of those tracks in figure 4.3 and write a succinct analysis suggesting why the playwright would have specified the styles he did at particular moments in the drama. Do you hear any correlation between the text content and the way the text is performed?

Another important element in *nō* performing style is the type of rhythmic relationship called for between the text delivery and the accompanying instruments. There are two types:

• *Au*, congruent rhythm, in which the rhythm of the chanting and the rhythm of the drums "matches."

• *Awazu*, noncongruent, in which that rhythm does not "match." The rhythms in the vocal and drum parts are independent.

On CD track 3, at 0:14, the chorus sings in the melodic "soft-singing" style a subsection called *sageuta* that emphasizes the low pitch area. The placement of the eleven syllables (each shown in figure 4.3 as 7 + 4) in each line is closely coordinated with the drum rhythm, in congruent rhythm (*au*). At 0:43 the texture shifts in a subsection called *kuri*. The singing style does not change but the text-syllable-to-drum-rhythm relationship does; it is noncongruent rhythm (*awazu*).

A moment in the play when the nature of the congruent rhythm is utterly clear is the climactic ending chorus, a subsection called *noriji* in which the vocal and drum parts match in the one-syllable-to-one-beat system (CD track 22, after 4:03).

The Acting Forces. The number of actors (all male) in any play is relatively small. Rather than thinking of them as individual characters, the actors are first identified by the role type:

• The *shite* (pronounced "shtay," rhyming with "they") role is the principal character. There are now five hereditary lineages of *shite* actors—Kanze, Hosho, Komparu, Kongo, and Kita.

• The *waki* role is the second main character; in many plays the role is just as important as the *shite*. There are three *ryū* of *waki* actors—Hosho, Fukuo, and Takayasu.

• *Kyōgen* roles depict other individual characters. In some plays (but not in *Ataka*) a *kyōgen* is humorous and can even improvise humorous lines. There are two schools of *kyōgen* actors—Okura and Izumi.

• *Tsure* are supporting roles, usually a group allied with either the *shite* or *waki* character. They are performed by *ryū* actors in training for the main roles.

• *Kokata* is a role of a child, played by a child actor.

Each *ryū* focuses on some of the extant repertoire of about 250 plays. The recordings of *nō* on the CD were made by actors of the Kita *ryū* that performs *Ataka* (figure 4.6). When a play is in the repertoire of more than one *ryū*, slight changes in text are made, and the movement styles and staging differ somewhat, resulting in a group's version of the play.

In *Ataka* most of the characters are associated with the fleeing Minamoto band, as follows. The *samurai* retainer Benkei is the *shite* role, while his young Minamoto warrior lord, Yoshitsune, is cast as a *kokata* (to suggest perhaps the reduced state the former hero was in at that point in his life). Nine *samurai* followers are *tsure*, and a lowly baggage carrier (*gōriki*) for the group is a *kyōgen* character. Togashi, the chief officer at the barrier, is the *waki* and he has one supporter, a swordbearer in the *waki-tsure*-role.

FIGURE 4.6 *Recording session for CD examples of* nō Ataka *at Kita Nogakudo, Tokyo, May 2002. From left to right: Mitsuo Kama (ō-tsuzumi); Shingo Ko (ko-tsuzumi); Richard Emmert (nōkan); Shinya Inouye; Sadamu Omura; and Daisaku Tani, actors.*

ACTIVITY 4.3 *To review the* Ataka *tale, reread figure 4.3. Find the line "treading on the tale of a tiger" and write a short statement about the meaning of it in this story.*

Movement.   Motion in *nō* is so stylized, so slow, and pared to such a minimum that each movement carries a tremendous effect. Sliding the feet, with the body held in a certain stance particular to the *ryū*, actors glide for the most part rather than walk or run. The occasional leap is startling; even a single stomp is dramatic; the word "dance" seems an exaggeration even for the portions of a play that are designated as such (e.g., the *Ataka no mai,* at 3:28 on CD tracks 22 and the entirety of track 23). Movements are suggestive rather than realistic, such as the hand lifted to the face to represent the loyal Benkei's crying after he has had to beat his lord, Yoshitsune. When the *shite* wears a mask, the total effect seems otherworldly. Yet somehow, intense drama is imparted. The *nō* is a theater of allusion, without the intention of realistic portrayal.

The Musicians and Instruments.   Important in every *nō* play is a chorus, consisting of actors in the troupe who are not playing a role at the time. At the beginning of a performance, as the instrumentalists enter along the walkway at stage left, the chorus comes onstage through a low door at rear stage right; a Buddhist symbol of humility, they must stoop to pass through. The men kneel on the stage floor in two rows along stage right, facing center stage; the leader is unidentifiable in the back row. The chorus sometimes speaks for an actor, sometimes narrates. This will be clear to you if you find the chorus sections in figure 4.3 and analyze the function of the chorus in each instance.

By now you will have understood that *nō* actors are musicians and dancers as well as actors, in that they sing as well as speak, dance as well as move. A smooth flow among those elements is part of what defines the theatrical style.

Three drums and a flute comprise the instrumental ensemble, or *hayashi* (figure 4.7). Signaling the beginning of a performance, the musicians enter along the walkway, solemnly carrying their instruments. Throughout the performance they will be in view at the rear of the stage.

The *taiko* (a generic term for drum) is used exclusively for dance scenes. The *nō taiko* does not resemble the *gagaku taiko*. This one is small and barrel-shaped, suspended by ropes from a low lacquered stand. Kneeling on the floor, the player wields a heavy wooden stick in each hand, using dramatic motions that appear to be choreographed. Largely because the sounds from his strokes on the top head are resonated by the enclosing bottom head, and also because of the proximity to the wooden floor, the drum produces a remarkably loud sound for its size. At climactic moments in some plays, the *taiko* adds considerably to the drama. Although there is a climactic dance in *Ataka*, the *taiko* is not played, but you can hear it in an excerpt from the play *Hagoromo* on CD track 24.

The other two drums are *tsuzumi*, the name referring to the waisted shape of drum, similar to the *san no tsuzumi* of *gagaku*. The players of these drums sit on camp stools they have carried onstage with them. The *ko-tsuzumi* (literally "small drum"), is held over the player's left shoulder by his left hand and struck by the right hand. There are five basic sounds produced, onomatopoetically named *pon, pu, ta, chi,* and *tsu*. The heavier *ō-tsuzumi* ("big drum") is held resting on the player's

FIGURE 4.7 *Instruments of the* nō hayashi. *Left:* Taiko. *The two heads are made of either horse or cow skin, thicker top head. Patches of deerskin on center of the top skin controls sound somewhat. The rope system is very tight; one set holds skins to the body, the other encircles the drum. Middle:* Ō-tsuzumi. *Cowhide skins, with front head slightly thicker than rear. For high, hard sound, skins are heated and dried before every performance, and a freshly prepared drum may be brought to the player during performance. Two sets of rope lash the heads on tightly. A third rope is decorative, draped from the drum toward the floor. Right:* Ko-tsuzumi. *The body of zelkova wood is carved inside to improve the sound. Horsehide skins are stretched over iron rings, stitched at the rear with hemp thread, and lacquered. A small patch of deerskin is placed in the inside center of the back skin to control reverberation and therefore tone. Small patches of paper are applied to the outside of the rear skin immediately opposite the inner patch and reapplied for each use. Heads are loosely lashed and need moisture to create a fuller, reverberating sound. Players can be seen blowing on the heads to moisten them. Front:* Nōkan. *Among flutes, the nōkan has one unique feature: rather than producing a higher-octave when overblown, it overblows a little flat owing to the insertion inside of a thin tube between the lip hole and first finger hole. The tube also upsets the normal acoustical properties of the flute, producing a sound quality unique to nō. (Photo by Shinji Aoki.)*

left hip. He strikes it with one to three fingers of his right hand; he might cover his fingers with a thimble of hard paper to produce dryer, more cracking sounds or a thimble of deerskin for a softer tone. The basic sounds of each drum are spoken with syllables for learning (see activity 4.4).

Each drum's part consists of patterns. Unlike *gagaku* patterns, which are essentially the result of playing techniques, the *nō* patterns are learned rhythm patterns that are named. As in *gagaku* and *matsuri bayashi*, however, the drummers coordinate with each other, complementing or interlocking. Two factors complicate *nō* drumming: each of several *ko-tsuzumi* and *ō-tsuzumi ryū* has a version of the patterns. Furthermore, the "beat" is often flexible. Since rehearsals are uncommon, it can be quite a challenge to coordinate in performance.

Of considerable importance are calls (*kakegoe*) of the drummers—sometimes eerie, sometimes urgent, sometimes quiet, sometimes intense. Enunciated more or less as "ya," "a," "ha," "yo," "iya" (cueing a cadence), the calls are part of the rhythm patterns, permitting the drummers and actors to coordinate through the flexible beats. You can hear this in isolation on CD track 23, moments from a warmup session just before the *nō* selections for this book were recorded. The flute player sings his part, while the drummers speak the *kakegoe* and imitate strokes with a closed fan. In the performed play, the *kakegoe* function dramatically, even psychologically, as well. The contribution they make to the texture of the sound in *nō* cannot be overstated.

The flute (*nōkan*), the only melodic instrument in *nō*, is used in purely instrumental entrance music that begins plays and in instrumental dance segments such as *Ataka no mai*, as well as in vocal subsections. It, too, plays set patterns, but its set patterns are treated improvisationally when the rhythm is unmatched (*awazu*) to that of the drums. The flute melody has no specific pitch relationship with the melody of the singing. (This should not be surprising, since vocal pitch is treated so flexibly.) In any case, the deliberate clouding of almost every pitch in *nōkan* performance makes the label "pitch area" more meaningful than "pitch." Players learn the flute part through mnemonic syllables that you can hear being sung on CD track 23. The syllables are not pitch names but rather suggest the pitch relationships in a note cluster; the vowels indicate relative level of pitch, from higher to lower—*i, a, o, u*. In line 1 of figure 4.8, "o hya, o hya ri ya" includes *o, a, o, a, i,* and *a* in that order; *o* is the lowest pitch, *hya* in the middle, with *ri* just above *hya*. The actual pitches are relative and are ornamented in formal performance.

FIGURE 4.8 *The flute* (nōkan) *part at the beginning of* Ataka no mai. *(Courtesy of Richard Emmert.)*

ACTIVITY 4.4

• Listen first to the flute part of the *Ataka no mai*, following it on CD track 23. It is sung with mnemonic syllables first. In line 2 in figure 4.8, the first "hya" occurs at 0:23. A pattern that will repeat begins at 0:27; it begins again at 0:35.

• The performed flute part begins at 1:09; the repetition from line 3 begins at 1:38. It slows at 2:03 to go on to new material.

• Now focus on figure 4.9. You must shift your reading orientation from the horizontal staff notation to vertical Japanese notation. Begin at the top right corner and count down from beat 1 to beat 8. Without trying to read any detail, listen to all of CD track 23 just to feel the pulsation that becomes regular at about the beginning of column 2 (0:15). Put your finger on the horizontal line of each beat (1 to 8) and proceed from top to bottom, from right to left columns.

• Locate on figure 4.9 the flute mnemonic syllables you have learned from figure 4.8. They are written in the middle of each vertical column: column 1 "o hya, o hya, ri ya" and so forth. Then follow the flute part again on CD track 23.

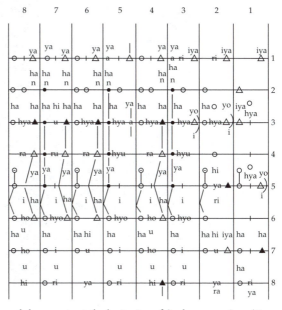

FIGURE 4.9   *The flute and drum parts at the beginning of* Ataka no mai.   *(Courtesy of Richard Emmert.)*

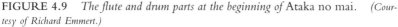

> • The *ō-tsuzumi* patterns (*kakegoe* calls and strokes) are written to the right side of each vertical column in figure 4.9. The *ko-tsuzumi* patterns are to the left. Follow each of them, if you can. If you cannot, just take note in the notation of how the patterns of the two drums interlock, how the *kakegoe* are part of the pattern, and how complex this seemingly transparent music is. CD track 23 is just a portion of the *Ataka no mai.*

ACTIVITY 4.5   *To review what you have learned about the* nō *drama, reread figure 4.3. Listen closely again to each selection on the CD as it comes in the play, following the Japanese text.*

This discussion of the *nō* drama and specifically of *Ataka* has prepared you to study the recurrence and transformation of textual and musical material in the *kabuki* play *Kanjinchō* and in the film *Men Who Step on the Tiger's Tail*.

THE *KABUKI* THEATER

From humble, even disreputable beginnings, *kabuki* theater was part of the world of sensual entertainment provided in the cities for the pleasure of the commoners. It is said to have begun with a woman—Okuni, an itinerant dancer who claimed association with Izumo Shrine and who, in 1603 or perhaps earlier, performed suggestive dances and skits in the dry bed of the Kamo River in Kyoto. Erotic and promiscuous associations continued as dance and skits turned from occasional entertainment to theater. The origins of *kabuki*, then, were linked to both male and female prostitution, and although the government repeatedly attempted to forge clear separations between the two professions by banning both women and homosexuals from the stage in the mid-seventeenth century, the distinction of function was not always clearly drawn. The theatrical and prostitution quarters became parallel facilities for amusement—the two wheels of the vehicle of pleasure, so to speak, tolerated but controlled by the government in the conviction that vulgar diversions for the lower classes, unprepared by education or lineage for more refined recreation, were necessary. It was argued that while the three great cities of Edo, Osaka, and Kyoto were under Tokugawa control, they would lose their commanding positions in population and hence in commerce without the presence of lively amusement areas. The audience of "commoners" included many wealthy but nevertheless low-status merchants. (Social status and economic status had little to do with each other in Tokugawa Japan. At the highest level were the impoverished courtiers, in the middle were many ranks of *samurai* from rich to poor, and at the bottom were merchants and other laborers.) The two professions, therefore, received some official recognition insofar as they were licensed by the *samurai* government and relegated to separate quarters, removed from the rest of society, and treated as analogous groups of pariahs (Shively 1978: 3).

In the all-male *kabuki* troupes, women's roles were played by specialist actors (*onnagata*) who held an erotic fascination for both men and women in the large audiences they attracted. "In a society in which there was an easy acceptance of homosexual relations, the presence of actors on the stage who deliciously exploited sexual nuance occasioned far more excitement than it does today." Most *kabuki* plays are about the lives of commoners, and seeing their lives so dramatized, "commoners found [all the actors] endlessly fascinating, admiring them for their beauty and their splendid clothes, their social poise and savoir faire" (Shively 1978: 4) A real-life scandal could provide the basis for a new play within days. Such was the case with a double love-suicide; so popular did one *kabuki* play become that it inspired a rash of additional double love-suicides.

In fact, however, *samurai* as well as commoners flocked to *kabuki*, and eighteenth-century theaters in Edo provided relatively private boxes for high-status women, members of the Buddhist clergy, and rich merchants. This was popular culture, in the literal sense. The wide embrace of the entire entertainment industry can be glimpsed through the production and sale of woodblock prints depicting the theater interiors, teahouses attached to the theaters, famous actors (figures 1.4 and 4.10), and stylish *geisha*. To the present, those prints are emblematic of Japanese traditional culture.

Kabuki became "classical" theater in the late nineteenth century when the connection with the pleasure quarters (the "floating world") ended and *kabuki* actors, whose private lives became quite different, were elevated to the status of artists. The "classical" repertoire consists of plays but also of dance pieces that recall the earlier ambiance in an elegant fashion. Acting in the *onnagata* roles became more and more a style of formalized grace, singling out those most essential traits of a woman's gestures and speech. What is important is not the gender of the actor but the representation of gender through acting skills. Hereditary and adoptive lineages of actors (i.e., houses such as the Ichikawa and Nakamura families) through many generations have maintained precious traditions as skills are passed from older members of a family of actors to younger. In 1969 the National Theater established the Kabuki Actor Training Center to teach aspiring performers from outside the *kabuki* world as well; it gets them started with two years of instruction.

From Nō *to* Kabuki. Woodblock prints and scroll paintings permit us to trace the adoption into *kabuki* of many traits of *nō*. The early *kabuki* stage basically recreated the square *nō* stage with pillars in the four corners supporting a roof, spaces to side and rear for musicians, and the "bridge" for entrances and exits. The musical ensemble was the *nō hayashi* of drums and flute. And, significantly, *nō* plays were taken into the repertory and adapted to *kabuki* performance style. Theater

FIGURE 4.10   *Contemporary woodblock print of Benkei reading the subscription list.   (Courtesy of the artist, Hotsuka Toyokuni.)*

managers and actors, after all, wanted to appeal to their audiences, and men and women of the upper classes were there. Particularly in the third month of the year, ladies-in-waiting from the *shōgun's* castle and the lord's mansions in Edo, and from the imperial palace in Kyoto, received vacation time to visit their families, "but many headed straight for the theater. Plays were often scheduled during that month on themes drawn from classical literature appropriate to this clientele" (Shively 1978: 29). Among them was *Ataka*, which was transformed into *Kanjin-chō* by the playwright Namiki Gohei III (1789–1855) (Scott 1953:11) and the *nagauta* musician Rokusaburo Kineya IV (1780–1855).

Soon in the history of *kabuki*, further stylistic distinctions between it and the *nō* developed. The size of the stage and therefore the size of the casts were gradually increased. In the process of modernizing, proscenium stage design with its lighting, sets, and curtain systems was adopted for *kabuki*. The *nō* theater walkway to the side of the stage was replaced by the *hanamichi*, a five-foot-wide walkway extending from the left side of the stage through the audience to a small enclosure at the rear of the theater through which the actors appear and disappear. Because flamboyant or intense moments—including entrances, exits, and *mie*, striking poses held for dramatic effect and admiration—take place on it, seats in full view of the *hanamichi* were and are the most desirable. Audience response has always been both spontaneous and encouraged; you can hear spontaneous applause on CD track 25 at 0:24 and near the end. A custom that continues to the present is a sudden and startling shout from an enthusiastic viewer (or theater plant) to applaud an especially skillful pose or vocal coloration in the delivery of a dramatic line. A fan might call out the actor's name or his house name (CD track 15 just after 1:07 and 1:27).

Kanjinchō.   *Kanjinchō* was first performed in its present form in March 1840 by the actor who later took the stage name of Danjuro Ichikawa VII (1791–1859), in commemoration of his illustrious forefather Danjuro Ichikawa I (1660–1704). The role of Benkei became associated with the Ichikawa lineage. When *kabuki* was performed before an emperor for the first time in 1887, the play was *Kanjinchō* and Benkei was performed by Danjuro Ichikawa IX (1838–1903) (Scott 1953: 12). (In the selections on the CD with this book, Danjuro Ichikawa XI plays the leading role.) Since the piece entered the canon of eighteen grand spectacle plays that was established in the nineteenth century, the story has had its most frequent performances in *kabuki* style. It is now the exemplar for *kabuki* in public school textbooks; without women characters, there is no risk of suggesting immorality or even the risqué past of the theatrical genre.

The Musicians.   Most important to note here are two differences from *nō* in the sphere of music. One is the use of instruments for sound effects and also for intertextual references (as defined in the citation that begins this chapter). Behind a shuttered wall at stage left, musicians can see the stage but are hidden from the audience in a special room (*geza*). Coordinating with action onstage, for example, a *koto* is played to reference elite culture when an event in a palace or castle is mentioned. Impending suicide or some other tragedy is forecast by the slow beating of a large drum. *Matsuri bayashi* accompanies a scene at a shrine festival or generally brings gaiety and fun to mind. In some plays *geza* music is the only music specified for the production, while in others it complements an onstage ensemble. In still others (*Kanjinchō* among them), however, *geza* music is not a part of the texted soundscape.

Second, the origin of *kabuki* in popular culture is reflected in a body of singers and their *syamisen* accompanists who complement the instrumentalists of the *nō hayashi* to compose a full ensemble for *kabuki* music. A scene will call for one or more song genres—*tokiwazu* (CD track 7) or *nagauta* (the genre used in *Kanjinchō*), for example—depending on the mood and function of the music. Musicians specializing only in that genre will be scheduled to appear. Some plays (such as *Kanjinchō*) and dance pieces have such music from beginning to end. Others include it only in some scenes, while yet others do not include these formal *kabuki* musical genres at all.

Singers and *syamisen* players work in pairs, though you would not know it from the seating onstage—all singers to the left, all *syamisen* players to the right, often arrayed in full view in an elevated row across the rear of the stage. *Syamisen* players also work independently of the singers, punctuating lines spoken by actors, as the drummers do. Sparse *syamisen* accompanying one speaker can be amazingly effective, as when Yoshitsune, Benkei, and their men comment on their escape after the awful moment when Benkei has to beat his lord in an effort to convince Togashi that the porter is not Yoshitsune (figure 4.11, part 10 [on page 95], CD track 15). The complementarity between the quiet, slow *syamisen* melody and the vocal delivery of the actor is striking. Like drummers, *syamisen* players utter *kakegoe*; this can be heard, for example in the singer's line in part 6, CD track 26, at 1: 42, "Takaraka ni koso," "Loudly he reads."

ACTIVITY 4.6 *Read* Kanjinchō *as encapsulated in figure 4.11 and compare the text to that of* Ataka *in figure 4.3. I have provided the full* kabuki *text only where at least part of the section is performed on a CD selection. When the recording does not begin at the first line of a section, an asterisk marks the beginning.*

• Find the references to the recorded portions of *Kanjinchō* in figure 4.11 and photocopy the texts.

• Listen to CD tracks 15 and 25–29. Note on the text not only where (a) the *syamisens*, (b) drums, and (c) flute are heard but also precisely where they start and stop. This will give you a good sense of the use of the instruments in the dramatic pacing and texture of the *kabuki* performing style.

The singers in *kabuki* music are not actors as they are in *nō*; they are professional musicians. If a play has been adapted from *nō*, those singers will present the chorus sections and also replace the singing that *nō* actors would have done. The singing plays just as important a dramatic role in *kabuki* as in *nō*. A good example of this is the drinking scene in part 12 (CD track 28), in which the music creates a kind of polyvocality by expressing something different from what is being acted out. While the staged drinking scene exudes some humor and increasing exaggerated drunkenness (audible in the recording because it is from a live performance), the *nagauta* singers reveal what is really in Benkei's mind—remembrance of his only love. This song is not in the *nō* text; it is an addition that the pleasure-quarter audience of Tokugawa period Edo would have relished.

ACTIVITY 4.7 *Listen to CD tracks 15 and 25–29 and focus particularly on the parts where the text is rendered by the na-gauta singers. Listen closely to CD track 28 (part 12 in figure 4.11) to hear how the lines are sung by different singers.*

Write an analysis of the role of the singers (together, or as single voices) in these recordings. Do they act as narrator (storyteller) or commentator, for instance? Are they performing text that is different or the same as the nō *text? What is their melodic relationship with the* syamisen?

Singing skills are not required of *kabuki* actors, but they nonetheless cultivate dramatic use of the voice and also extravagant, flamboyant movement—the exact opposite of *nō* style. Benkei's acting in the line "Omoeba, nikushi, nikushi' in part 9 (CD track 25 at 0:15) is a good example of the manly *aragoto* style, when the actor struts and milks the text for all it is worth. The amount of action and the size of the cast create a very different theatrical effect from the restrained, minimalist *nō*. Appropriately for the wide proscenium stage, Togashi's one swordbearer in *Ataka* is expanded by a whole group of guards. Although in *Kanjinchō* the restrained robes of the wandering monks are replicated from *Ataka*, in many *kabuki* plays costuming and facial makeup contribute to creating an effect that is larger than life.

The Music. With additional acting and musical forces, the intertextual process of adapting a *nō* play to *kabuki* style results in a fascinating mix and match of old text and new, old music and new, restrained *nō* performance style and flamboyant *kabuki*. As you can see and hear following figure 4.11 at part 2 and CD track 27, the transformation is evident from early in *Kanjinchō*. The instrumental entry music at the beginning of part 2 is imitative of *nō* but not adopted precisely. It properly begins with a shrill flute blast that unmistakably announces the beginning of a play. Also properly, the drums start out with uneven "beats" and elongated vocal calls of the drummers (*kakegoe*); they are approximating *nō* patterns. The *nagauta* singers render the opening poem of *Ataka* with "choral" *tsuyogin*-like vocal delivery, accompanied on drums by an imitation congruent (*au*) pattern. Thus the intertextual use of the *nō* text is literal but use of the music is referential. That quickly gives way to a declaration that this is *kabuki*, with entry of the popular-culture *syamisen*. Though the text of the next song (from "Toki shimo") is from *Ataka*, this music is *nagauta* style—melodically, and with *syamisen* enhancement of both the song and the action (the typical traveling pattern after "tachi idete" at 3:07 for instance). Lots of the characteristic up-down "*chiri kara*" *syamisen* stroking pattern is heard here.

In the final scene of the play, all the *kabuki* theatrical forces are brought together, with the text straight from *Ataka*. Benkei dances at Togashi's request and we hear reference to the *nō* *Ataka no mai* in the first fifty seconds of CD track 29 (see activity 4.4). However, the spirit of Tokugawa-era popular culture takes over as the drummers, *syamisen* players, and singers launch into the *nagauta* *chirashi* and *dangire* musical sections from the last "*Naru wa taki no mizu.*" Suddenly, Benkei has lifted his fan and given a hasty signal behind it for his party to leave; they rise and prepare to depart hurriedly while he is still dancing. The text ends with the chorus expressing this for all: "feeling they trod a tiger's tail."

The rhythmic notation for this climactic ending is shown in figure 4.12. It consists of two *nagauta* sections—*chirashi* and *dangire*. A few notes

FIGURE 4.12 *Rhythmic notation of the* chirashi *and* dangire *sections at the end of* Kanjinchō. *(Courtesy of John Lytton (Tasajo Mochizuki).)*

(continued)

FIGURE 4.12 *Continued.*

(continued)

FIGURE 4.12 *Continued.*

FIGURE 4.12 *Continued.*

will help you read the notation (John Lytton: personal communication, 2003):

- The vocal part does not follow the rhythm of the accompaniment closely. There is a fair amount of variation in performance. Therefore only text is shown. Find the *chirashi* section in figure 4.11, part 12 to orient yourself.
- *Syamisen* rhythm, not pitch, is notated, because that is how the drummers orient to it.
  The *v* denotes an upstroke of the plectrum.
  The upside down *u* denotes left-hand pizzicato (finger pluck).
  The word "hammer" denotes sounding the note by pressing the finger on the string.

- *Ko-tsuzumi*
  The *x* denotes a higher sound (played while tightening ropes).
  The *o* denotes a deeper sound (relaxing the ropes). A filled circle is one beat, an empty one is two beats.

- *Ō-tsuzumi* (ōkawa)
  A filled triangle denotes a shorter, softer sound, an open triangle a longer, louder sound.

As in the *nō* drumming at this point, short patterns are repeated to comprise the section. *Nagauta* drummers learn the patterns through syllables, referring to the *syamisen* rhythm as well. The three patterns in *chirashi* in figure 4.12 begin from the text "Hi wa teru tomo," and occur as follows:

- *Chiri kara chiri toto* | *tsuta tsuta tsu   tton* (played eleven times)
- *Cho   cho   ta   ta* | *tsuta tsuta tsu   ta* |*pon tsuta tsu ton* | *tsuta tsuta tsu tton* (played three times)
- The first pattern is played again three times.
- *Cho cho ta   ta* | *chiri kara tsu   ta* | *pon* | *ta*
- "I ya" is the cue for the cadential *dangire* pattern.

ACTIVITY 4.8 *Speak the* chirashi *and* dangire *patterns until they become easy to do at a fairly rapid pace. Then you should be able to follow them on the recording, CD track 29, from 2:22.*

"The play" ends with the dramatic departure of the actors and especially Benkei. At 3:43 on CD track 29 you can hear the unmistakable clear sound of the woodblocks that announce the beginning and end of plays. The curtain has been pulled across the stage to hide the scenery, but his men and lastly Benkei are still making their way down the *hanamichi* walkway through the audience.

As you can see from this look at *Ataka* and *Kanjinchō*, the intertextual process resulted in two very different productions based on some of the same material. This is quite different from a production of a Shakespeare play, for instance, that is updated in setting, costuming, and provided with music. There, the text is the thing, and beyond modernizing the English language, little tampering is tolerated.

ACTIVITY 4.9 *Focus on the intertextual process in this chapter has led you to concentrate on similarities. Now shift your attention and write an essay comparing* Ataka *and* Kanjinchō, *giving specific examples of how the two performance styles differ.*

THE FILM *MEN WHO STEP ON THE TIGER'S TAIL*

As Kurasawa's film *Men Who Step on the Tiger's Tail* opens, our band of "monks" in robes familiar from the *nō* and *kabuki* costumes are on their way somewhere, true to the structure of an opening scene of *a nō* drama. Specifically, they are making their way on a mountain trail. We hear bells in the distance, referencing the many temples the men would have been passing in the old Heike stories. Most telling in intertextual terms, we are also hearing a chorus of male singers (CD track 30). The opening poem is from the plays and, indeed, the chorus starts out in chantlike style, recalling the *nō*. The first seven-plus-five syllable line is sung only once, however, and the unison melody of the second line does not resemble *tsuyogin*. Interesting here is the way in which the composer, Tadashi Hattori, maintains the idea of the asymmetrical Japanese structure, even though the supporting ensemble is the European orchestra. The total effect of this brief intertextual moment is a sense of the uncertainty the men must have been feeling.

The *gōriki* plays a real role in the film version. He has been hired locally and is acting informally as a guide. The lowly porter has no idea whom he is guiding, and when he attempts to make small talk the men react with irritation. At the song of a nightingale (an intertextual reference to the noble home Yoshitsune has left), they stop to rest. Their conversation alludes to the Yoritomo-Yoshitsune struggle and the setting up of a barrier. As they discuss their plan for getting through the barrier, the porter eavesdrops and finally realizes who they are. The comedian-actor Enoken reacts with exaggerated fright. He hears that they have decided to disguise Yoshitsune as a *gōriki*.

In neither *Ataka* nor *Kanjinchō* was attention given to Yoshitsune's donning his disguise, so this is new dramatization. We can now tell that in this film he is played by an adult actor as in the *kabuki*. The change is portrayed with elegant weight, accompanied by male and female vocalists, singing a distinctive, rhetorically Japanese melody but with European vocal technique. First they sing in alternation, then together, with poetic references and expressions of deep pity for the young lord.

MALE SINGER: The startling beauty of a crimson blossom [referring to Yoshitsune] is seen even in a garden laden with flowers.

FEMALE SINGER: Yet lesser blossoms are overlooked and weeds unnoticed. And so he removed his brocade coat, putting on the porter's coarser weave.

TOGETHER: The sight of the spent, bending lord who had never carried a load before is painful to look upon, and we must sigh with grief.

As the men ready themselves to travel on, the porter wants to stay with them, but they send him back. Without pack now, he follows, then disappears, and the men tromp through woods. Then the *gōriki* laughingly reappears, but they still ignore him pridefully. "What shall we do? We shall not ask a commoner for favors." Persisting, the *gōriki* reappears again, and finally the men ask him about the barrier. When he replies that the guards expect them, the men report to Benkei. The men want to fight their way through, but Benkei worries about barriers yet to come and tells them that they will pretend to be traveling to collect funds to rebuild the Todaiji temple at Nara.

The *nō hayashi* introduces the scene at the barrier, where they meet Togashi and his men. Benkei explains who they are and why they are there; in the exchange between Benkei and Togashi, some lines are taken from the *kabuki* text. The "monks" are told that they must not resist. Benkei just sits quietly and inquires why they would kill real Buddhist priests for no reason.

At this point in the film, a character is introduced who was in neither *Ataka* nor *Kanjinchō*, though he is in the old Heike stories. Kagetoki
Kajiwara is said to have slandered Yoshitsune to Yoritomo, thus causing the rift between the two brothers. Some of Togashi's more aggres-
sive, challenging lines have thus been given to Kagetoki, and he is intent on killing anyone who might be Yoshitsune. Told to prepare
themselves for death, Benkei and his men silently turn their backs to
the threatening guards (and the camera). The rubbing of the rosaries is
enacted.

As we who know the story could predict, Togashi asks Benkei to
read from the subscription scroll. In a panic, the comic *gōriki* brings
Benkei a pack, from which Benkei removes a scroll. Any person in the
audience who does not know the story realizes from the porter's in-
discrete initial reaction that Benkei is "reading"—in *tsuyogin* style—
from nothing. The "reading" text (CD track 26) is the same as in the *nō*
but differs from the point at which that recording ends. Togashi's effort to see the text is thwarted, just as in the other two versions. Togashi
then asserts his authority and, as in the *kabuki* version, questions Benkei
at some length about his Buddhist sect: Why are there tassels on your
cap? Why do you carry your long stick, your sword? The background
sound is the full *nō hayashi*—until, that is, the climactic reference is made
to the precious secret nine-word prayer of the Shingon sect. The nine
words are spoken with the mighty orchestra.

Over the objection of Kagetoki, Togashi decides to act as if he believes they are not Yoshitsune's men. Kagetoki, however, sits and paces
in great frustration as Togashi has his men prepare gifts as contribution
to the temple. A men's chorus sings in unison, reiterating one pitch in
a kind of martial monophony accompanied by agitated strings: "Leave
as swiftly as you are able, but not so swiftly that you would appear less
innocent," and as the orchestra joins the monotone turns into a real
choral piece, "as though you tread upon the tail of the tiger." It is Kagetoki who yells: "Stop that man!" The comic *gōriki* stops, assuming he is
being rebuked. "No, not him—the other one!"

Sounds and Benkei's arm motions are all we see of the beating; this
is prolonged, relative to the time it gets in *nō* (where it is only a few
seconds) and in *kabuki* (only slightly longer, as if the heinous deed is
too painful to dwell on). The distressed *gōriki* tries to stop the beating.

Even after the beating, Kagetoki keeps up the challenge until Benkei
accuses him of wanting to steal the contents of Yoshitsune's pack. To
orchestral accompaniment, Benkei's men push back the border guards—
an action staged in both *Ataka* and *Kanjinchō*. Still, tenaciously Kagetoki

tries one further time to insist that they must not let the men go, but Togashi asserts that "no vassal would strike his own master." Benkei stands quietly, as unison melody in the orchestra escorts the band of "monks" from the barrier.

The scene changes to the countryside. The men laugh with relief and comment on how clever it was of Benkei to think of the plan; the *gōriki's* rejoinder is that he thought Benkei had suddenly lost his mind. Laughter stops, however, when they see Benkei, who kneels before Yoshitsune with head close to the ground and apologizes for "an unforgiveable sin, even if it was a desperate measure." At this moment, Yoshitsune is revealed full face for the first time; to a melody in flute and strings, with quiet, European-style orchestral accompaniment, Yoshitsune responds as he does in *Ataka* and *Kanjinchō*. This quiet, weighty scene is interrupted by the arrival of some of the guards from the barrier, bearing gifts of apology from Togashi. If you are able to view the movie, notice that the chief man looks over at Yoshitsune and starts to bow—obviously in recognition of who he is—but stops himself.

The now-familiar drinking scene ensues. A solo male song speaks of the "cup of friendship, taste of kindness." As the *sake* flows, we hear *matsuri bayashi* flute and drums; the drinking bowl becomes bigger, the pace accelerates, and the *gōriki* gets quite drunk. "Who will dance?" asks Benkei. The music stops abruptly. Benkei tells the *gōriki* to dance in celebration. Military music in brass and piccolo accompanies the porter's staggering until he passes out. Benkei: "I, too, will dance before I bid farewell." Unlike the other two versions, this is a short scene that only suggests the *Ataka no mai*. Those in the know would sense the approach of the end of the film, as we hear *tsuyogin*-like chanting to the familiar lines "*Naru wa taki no mizu. Naru wa taki no mizu. Hi wa teru tomo, taezu tōtari, taezu tōtari, taezu tōtari.*" The scene darkens, as the *nō hayashi* gives way to the sound of wind. Waking up, the *gōriki* finds himself alone; to the sound of *taiko* and the shrill *nō* flute (the sure signal of an ending), he "dances" away. The orchestra has the final sound, with a unison "Japanese melody" at the end.

In the music of *Men Who Step on the Tiger's Tail*, Tadashi Hattori substantiated the relationships between texts of Japanese traditional culture as he referenced *nō*-style vocal delivery, booming temple bells, *matsuri bayashi*, and melodies in a distinctive Japanese scale. He also substantiated relationships between texts of different cultures, as he drew on the European orchestra, military band music, harmonic hymn-like choral music, and solo vocal music with European aesthetic and technique. Akira Kurosawa—knowledgeable about Heike texts even beyond those of *Ataka* and *Kanjinchō*, and also about the potential for turning the *kyōgen* character of *Ataka* into a comic *kyōgen* role—continued in the contemporary medium of film the intertextual effort that has marked the Japanese arts through time. The historical depth and the rich repertoire of shared understanding on which the effort can draw make the Japanese practice quite remarkable.

In this chapter, I have explored three dramatic media to illustrate intertextuality in the theatrical arts. Intertextuality will reappear in the next chapter as well, embedded within continuing discussion of the theme of Japan's interface with other cultural spheres of the world.

CHAPTER 5

Managing International Interface

∞

As you now know well, Japan has experienced three periods of intense interactions with other cultural spheres. Each period has found that island culture in a different circumstance. In the first millennium emerging leaders were just in the process of creating a relatively unified political and cultural entity for the first time; in the nineteenth century a complex political and cultural system was in place, but it was one that, in the circumstances of worldwide economic and political colonialism, put the country at risk. At the beginning of the twenty-first century Japan is one of the world's most politically stable and economically powerful nations. In this chapter I shall continue the story of international interface in this latest period, then consider how the results of interface are being managed by musicians and institutions.

CONTINUING INTERFACE

Flushed with the rapid success of its modernizing process, and following the model of England—the most successful of the colonizers and a somewhat similar small island nation—Japanese imperialists set out early in the twentieth century to colonize their neighbors. By 1910 they were in control of Korea (see chapter 3 concerning Michio Miyagi). Ironically, it was the Japanese who introduced European music and its educational system into Korea, with effects on indigenous music there similar to those in Japan.

Early in Japan's Showa period (1926–89), with a spirit of supporting the work of musicians whose music education had been European, frequent contests promoting "nationalistic" music were sponsored by leading newspapers and music journals. Also fostering domestic artists, on 24 September 1931 Japanese national radio (NHK) presented the first program of European-style classical music by Japanese composers. To resist commercial domination and to limit the amount of European music that was aired, NHK began charging Western recording companies a high fee for the broadcast of each selection (Herd 1987: 30).

In the 1930s the voices of militancy and imperialist ambitions grew ever stronger, and "nationalism" took on different meanings. "The nation" began to turn its attention to colonizing China and also to marshalling the support of the citizenry against the competitor "West." By 1934 music books and recordings were heavily censored by the government, to a point where recordings in public libraries were taken from the shelves and strict time limits were set for listening. After the outbreak of full-scale war in China in July 1937, there was an almost complete ban of foreign musics except for classical music of their allies, Germany and Italy.

Several composers, record company producers, and officials from the Ministry of Information designed a plan to control the popular music industry as well. Some composers cooperated with the government, but others stopped composing (Herd 1987: 73). The ministry published a collection of nationalistic songs and produced more than 1 million records of them; six companies that cooperated with the government were allowed to distribute them.

In the 1930s as well, the government began to control closely all cultural education in public schools. After February 1936 the Ministry of Education actively used music as a tool for internal propaganda. Existing school songs were replaced temporarily with music for "entertainment" infused with patriotic and nationalistic themes: "virile songs" that were mainly *gunka* (war songs), military songs and marches, and other patriotic songs replaced American songs such as Stephen Foster's tunes and game songs (Herd 1987: 72).

Musicians with whom I have spoken remember other purposes that music in the schools was enlisted to serve. It came up, for example, in a 1999 interview with the composer Kikuko Masumoto about her early music education:

> I was born in 1937. [As a young child] I was studying ear training. You just memorized and guessed the pitch. . . . Small children are really good at ear training. It is easy to develop absolute pitch.
> When I was a child, World War II began. . . . Then military thought began. Oh—ear training. Do you know B-29? [I was slow to respond, because the conversation had taken an unexpected turn.] B-29 is an airplane, a bomber. It is the most famous name—B-29. Everyone knows it in Japan. When it comes overhead, you can tell. You can tell that one is Douglas, that one is B-29. That's what military officers

thought. So then they made all the children have ear training. Not only the people who studied music. Ordinary elementary school children were obligated to have ear training. So ear training became very feverish; everyone had to have it. . . . In Showa 19 [1945] every day, every day there were air attacks. It was the same as in Europe.

Also regarding air strikes, the composer Toshi Ichiyanagi remembers another function the government called on music to play. His father, a cellist, along with other musicians in the NHK Symphony Orchestra, were told to imitate the sounds of bombers with cello sounds in order to warn the populace of attacks. "Passing, the sound goes down. We had to be careful about approaching bombers—where was the plane. They were well imitated, for warning, on the radio" (personal communication, 23 May 2003).

The government also ordered all jazz bands, purveyors of the quintessential music of the enemy, to disband, but in reality that did not happen; a 1941 police document suggested how to use jazz rather than eradicate it. A genre called "light music" was created—the rhythm smoothed out, saxophones removed, bands enlarged on the model of orchestras (CD track 31). "Our present mission as a people is to build up a new Japanese culture by adopting and sublimating Western cultures with our national polity as the basis, and to contribute spontaneously to the advancement of world culture" (cited in Atkins 2001: 145–46). To survive, some jazz musicians played along, feeling that to create something new and positive, something relevant and unfrivolous yet popular and inspiring for a time of national crisis would be a positive contribution (Atkins 2001: 123, 152).

Bans against "undesirable music" must not have been altogether effective, because in 1943 the Information Bureau and Home Ministry reiterated the national campaign to "sweep away American and English music from our homes and streets." Partly to get rid of the equally undesirable English language of the enemy, record companies changed their names and even some instruments were renamed: the saxophone became *kinzoku seihin magari syakuhati* ("bent metallic flute") (Atkins 2001: 151). Several Japanese have mentioned to me that pitch names in "do re mi" solfège were replaced by Japanese syllables although "do re mi" syllables are European, not American.

After the war ended on 15 August 1945, the Japanese people quickly began accommodating to the occupation by American forces from 1945 to 1954. Controlling the media, the occupation authorities saturated the Japanese with Americana; jazz and baseball were encouraged, and

American films circulated widely. Censorship was instituted, and although its ideological aims differed from earlier Japanese censorship, it was in some ways just as severe. (Kurosawa's 1945 film *Men Who Step on the Tiger's Tail* was banned for five years.) Loyalty on the part of musicians to the old style of overt music nationalism would not be tolerated in the postwar period: "Attacks full of vengeance, justified by an aura of freedom and emboldened by anti-nationalist occupation forces, were printed in music journals and magazines for approximately one year after the end of the war," starting some bitter battles among composers (Herd 1987: 96).

Classical instrumental music, as a nontexted medium, escaped postwar censorship of the occupation authorities. Reflecting postwar politics, the leading composer Tomojiro Ikenouchi introduced music of an American ally, France, and the French conservatory system to Geidai, then Japan's most influential music school, to replace the German system. That influence remains strong to the present, with compositions by French composers such as Messiaen and Ravel receiving considerable programming time in numerous concerts. The time had passed, however, when European art musics were indiscriminately adopted as the preeminent models. "The main goal of fledgling composers was to create new, independent types of contemporary music that would simultaneously please the public and maintain high artistic standards worthy of international praise" (Herd 1987: 97). Among them were Toru Takemitsu and Minoru Miki, discussed in chapter 3.

Musicians in the popular sphere who had participated in the writing of Japanese-style "light music" during the war lost their chance for creativity, as troops in the American occupation forces wanted to be entertained by the music they would hear at home. The occupation period, the first opportunity they had for prolonged interaction with American musicians rather than learning from recordings or other foreigners, was at the same time a period when imitation was demanded. Furthermore, "because the essentially American character of jazz is regarded as so incontestable, Japan's jazz community has had to locate itself in an aesthetic hierarchy that explicitly reflects and reinforces asymmetries of power and cultural prestige on the Japan-US relationship by placing American artists at the apex as 'innovators' and non-Americans at the bottom as 'imitators' " (Atkins 2001: 11). Goodwill tours during the occupation and commercial tours in the 1960s kept American artists such as Dizzy Gillespie, Count Basie, and Louis Armstrong at the forefront of jazz in Japan.

The jazz scene flourishes in Japan today, populated by Japanese and foreign musicians. I shall discuss this further below.

Looking to the East. As Japan's economy improved and then boomed in the decades following "the Pacific war," postwar contacts with fellow Asian nations needed to be repaired and cultivated in different ways. This period coincided with the interest in what came to be called "world music," spurred by the growing field of ethnomusicology and with subsequent interest by the music industries. Resulting from both those forces and more recently from the whirlwind globalization of musical distribution systems, scholars and composers in Japan have found musics of other cultures to be of interest. International interface proceeds apace.

Among the composers who have referenced other Asian musics is Akira Nishimura (CD track 32; figure 5.1). As he related it to me, Nishimura was born 1953 in Osaka, at a time when Japan was still very poor. In Osaka it was difficult to study Western music—no violins, no piano; there was more traditional music there. He had heard European marches at school, but he was eleven years old before he touched his first LP (long-playing) record; hearing Beethoven's Ninth Symphony, he was "greatly affected" and requested his parents to buy him a phonograph, which they did at great sacrifice. His second request, at age twelve, was for a recording of Dvořák's *New World* Symphony; it came with a full score. "It blew me away that so many parts would be written by one person!" exclaimed Nishimura. Bypassing completely the usual next step of taking performing instruction, he asked his parents for composition lessons. They found a local high school teacher who was well connected, and in 1970, when an international exposition was held in Osaka, he was given an extraordinary opportunity. For six months there were ceremonies and concerts, and each pavilion had taped music for which leading composers were the directors; he was able to meet composers from Europe and America and Japan, among them Karlhaus Stockhausen (b. 1928) and Iannis Xenakis (b. 1922), whose influence is strong in Japan still.

By 1973 Nishimura was studying at Geidai with Tomojiro Ikenouchi, who had introduced French repertoire and pedagogy to Japan. In college, Nishimura experienced the boundaries among groups of composers in Japan—on one side, the academic composers who would have to do only with European music and, on the other side, composers such as Toru Takemitsu and Joji Yuasa (see below), whose more experimen-

FIGURE 5.1   *The composer Akira Nishimura, 1999.   (Photo by the author.)*

tal music was not tolerated by the other side. After graduating, Nishimura and friends formed the "Orchestra Project," a group without borders in terms of musical style.

Nishimura's musical flexibility continues to be a hallmark of his reputation as a composer. Mention of him in Japanese contemporary musical circles is likely to bring one of two immediate responses, one that notes how prolific he is, and the other that points out his interest in music of other Asian cultures. His lyrically melodic "Taqsim" for twenty-stringed *koto* (1982), for instance, develops the motive of the ubiquitous "Oriental scale" with reference to music of the Middle East. "Pipa" (1989) recalls the Chinese plucked lute. Several compositions are inspired by music of India, while "Ketiak" (1979; CD track 32) evokes Bali, where interlocking parts is a major musical practice (CD track 33).

ACTIVITY 5.1 *If you are not familiar with "Ketiak" (sometimes transliterated* ketchak*) of the Indonesian island of Bali, listen to CD track 33 (also see Gold 2005). The "percussive" men's group passages feature interlocking rhythms. Then listen to CD track 32 and write a brief statement about what you hear in it, relative to even the brief excerpt of Indonesian* ketiak/ ketchak *there. Do you hear solo-group contrasts, similar rhythmic textures, similar instrumentation, similar melody or tempo, for instance?*

Some Japanese jazz artists, too, have their ears open to other musics of Asia. The avant-garde saxophonist Sachi Hayasaka has been known to solo over Korean rhythmic patterns (*changdan*). The leader of the band Stir Up!, Hayasaka regards jazz as a music in which individual creativity is the only determining factor; to the historian Taylor Atkins she expressed bored frustration with the hang-ups over tradition, ethnic ownership, and authenticity that she believes actually dissipate the jazz world (2001: 274).

Niche Musics from Around the World. There are niche musics galore in Japan—ska, Bavarian folk song, bossa nova, blues, bluegrass, tango, and many others. Among them also is salsa; after a wildly successful tour through the United States in 1990, the Japanese band Orquesta de la Luz (CD track 34) ranked No. 1 on the Latin Salsa Chart in *Billboard* magazine for ten weeks in a row.

Writing about salsa, and specifically as performed by the Orquesta de la Luz, the anthropologist Shuhei Hosokawa observed: "The band has basically maintained a preference for the classic format of salsa, perfectly in line with the Japanese cultural hierarchy associated with niche musics" (1999: 516). Performers of niche musics in Japan, he says, choose to play the style as authentically as possible, that is, to reproduce an authentic sound, seldom injecting any Japanese features. Hosokawa suggests some intriguing reasons why Orquesta de la Luz would seek to reproduce an authentic sound rather than experiment within the genre or fuse it with others. (They took liberties with the texts, but not with the sound.) He takes the perspective of consumers, urbanites who are experiencing a sense of rootlessness as a result of the inexorable process of modernizing. Being alienated from the continuity of the indigenous tradition evokes in them a nostalgia for "roots music," music that is closely attached to the "heart" of the people. Having lost their own traditions, they search for the roots of the Other.

At the same time, one reason that Japanese audiences are especially receptive to Japanese musicians performing exotic music may be the country's relative ethnic homogeneity, he suggests. It allows Japanese to freely choose foreign music for performance or appreciate without questioning the racial and ethnic background of the artists. They are "color-blind" in the realm of aesthetic production. Moreover, the relatively large music markets in Japan allow ambitious musicians of niche genres to become professionals in Tokyo and Osaka (Hosokawa 1999: 521).

Why do Japanese fans seek roots music of others, rather than turning to their own music? "What matters for Japanese salsa musicians and audiences is the 'hipness,' the groove or the feeling of 'globality'; that is, the experience of listening or dancing to a faraway cultural product" (Hosokawa 1999: 516, 515). This is striking to me because, for most contemporary Japanese, *gagaku* and other *hōgaku* genres are "a faraway cultural product," distanced by time and experience. Perhaps some are turning to their own music for that very reason—to artists such as Hideki Togi, as discussed in chapter 3.

Another reason Hosokawa gives for Japanese musicians' concern for authenticity is that they want to maintain boundaries between "ours" and "theirs." Scholar after scholar has written about how important the maintenance of boundaries is in Japanese culture and society. Earlier, I mentioned one example, the situatedness of traditional cultural forms. The maintenance of group (*ryū*) and subgroup identities within one cultural form is another. The management of what has been adopted from others (a quintessentially Japanese mode of learning) has also called for the maintenance of boundaries. It can even be found in the language: a separate script (*katakana*) is used for writing foreign words, for instance. Since the Meiji period, a rhetorical paradigm of difference between *wayō* (Japanese style) and *seiyō* (Western style) has been deeply embedded in cultural expressions and thought.

Jazz and the Authenticity Issue.   Reflecting the *wayō-seiyō* bifurcation as a way of thinking, Japanese jazz by Japanese artists is likely to take a bad rap at home. The authoritative *Japan: An Illustrated Encyclopedia* neatly sums up the stereotypical dismissal; while this statement was written by a Western person, it was published by the eminent Japanese publishing firm Kodansha in a work meant to introduce international readers to their country:

One Western genre that has firmly established itself within the Japanese music scene is jazz. Japan is home to an important and highly profitable market for jazz, boasting numerous clubs, some of the best jazz magazines in the world, and a steady core of avid fans. Major international jazz figures play extensively in Japan's clubs and concert halls. The flourishing scene has also produced native musicians like saxophonist Watanabe Sadao, regarded as the patriarch of Japanese jazz, Hino Terumasa, and Watanabe Kazumi, and jazz fusion groups Casiopea and T Square. Yet while many of Japan's jazz artists display marvelous technical ability, few display any real originality. (Cahoon 1993: 1287)

In his thoughtful and well-documented study of jazz in Japan, E. Taylor Atkins explores the doubts that most Japanese jazz musicians express about their own lack of authenticity as makers of popular musical styles imported from abroad. No wonder, when they face this from prospective Japanese audiences, in stark contrast to the reception of niche musics. For audiences in Japan, jazz

> just doesn't seem "authentic" unless it is played by Americans. The craze is for performers from the U.S., who therefore naturally demand the highest prices they can get—much more, "sometimes ten times as much," than most could command in their own home country—and thereby drain the coffers of performance and recording fees that might go to Japanese musicians. . . .
>
> The paucity of jobs and money fosters a strange irony in which young Japanese musicians leave the richest jazz market in the world—Japan—to find work and to study in America, home of the musicians who are making all the money. (*Japan Update*, 1989, cited in Atkins 2001: 41)

The authenticity issue, expressed as "music being done right," has arisen in my conversations with Japanese consumers of classical music as well. Reading in a popular source of information about Japan that the two most frequently performed pieces of European music were Beethoven's Symphony No. 9 (see chapter 1) and Vivaldi's *Four Seasons* (see below), I went searching in Tokyo stores for recordings of them: of fifty-four choices for the Beethoven, I found only two recordings by Japanese orchestras (CD track 4 is an excerpt from one of them). Whereas I found only three CDs of the Vivaldi performed by Japanese musicians (CD track 1), I read in the same source that the rendition by the European orchestra I Musici had by 1996 sold 2.8 million copies in Japan (Inoue, Ozawa, Sakon, and Hosaka, 1996). "Why would this be?"

I have asked. "If it's going to be done right, it should be done by European musicians. Japanese like imported things," has come the response. There are probably more Japanese recordings of those two pieces than I found. However, the number of touring European orchestras, chamber music groups, opera companies, and soloists on Japanese concert programs is simply amazing, given the huge investment in specialized musical training and high level of accomplishment by Japanese musicians who specialize in those repertoires themselves. My annual visits to stores selling recordings show no change: those by Japanese artists must be searched for on the shelves, no matter what the international genre. The music is in the hearts of Japanese music lovers, but domestic professional performance of it appears to be accorded only second rank to that of foreigners.

Jazz musicians and Japanese consumers of European classical music, then, seem to share a concern about authenticity. (I have not yet asked professional Japanese performers of classical music about this.) No doubt it is not entirely an authenticity issue. Perhaps it is also a kind of exoticism—that "liking of imported things." Perhaps it is a way Japanese enjoy participating in international life.

Hip-hop in Japan.   The reception of hip-hop seems familiar in some ways, but also different from that of niche musics and jazz. "The invasion of sickening commercialism of Japanese popular culture": That's what some rappers thought of million-selling J-rap hits in the 1994–97 hip-hop boom (Condry 2001: 233). Better the music stay on recordings by independent labels, say Condry's informants, and cloistered in all-night dance clubs where the emotional intensity and energy of the music can really be felt, where different styles can emerge and even improvisation can be tried. There is little concern here about reproducing an authentic sound, and little way to avoid "injecting Japanese features."

It is the club scene that makes Japanese rap particularly meaningful. A significant reason should sound familiar to you now: the social organization of the Japanese hip-hop scene is best characterized as loose groups of "families" (*famirii*) who come together regularly at different club events. A family is a collection of rap groups, usually headed by one of the more famous Tokyo acts, with a number of protégés. These families arise primarily from the club scene and are the key to understanding stylistic differences between groups. By the late 1990s each of these groups had built up a following of its own, organized separate club events, and amassed a group of like-minded performers, so that distinctive styles have gradually coalesced around the central artists. There are strong affinities among groups that perform regularly together and marked differences between the different collectives (Condry 2001: 237–38). Now rap groups are becoming popular through recordings as well, most notably Zebra and Dragon Ash.

Catching on first among relatively affluent youth gathered in Yoyogi Park at Harajuku (see chapter 1), breakdancing boomed in Japan after the movie *Flashdance* showed in Tokyo in the summer of 1983. Gradually other characteristics of hip-hop—gear, DJing, rap, and graffiti—appeared, in roughly that order. Rapping presented particular challenges. Without much, if any, sense of African American ghetto life, without a poetic tradition of rhyming or even a language characterized by accentuation, but with a cultural etiquette of politeness, rap seemed unlikely to catch on. Nevertheless, it did, and by 2001 more than thirty Japanese-language rap groups had been signed with record labels and stars were hitting the international circuits.

Rap in Japan is not a music of the marginalized, but in a sense rappers are taking an important aspect of the music—association with social struggle—and localizing it. "When You the Rock considers oppression in a Japanese context, he does not say he suffered from racial discrimination, but rather that his family was looked down on in the neighborhood because of a chaotic home life (hot-tempered parents, many stepsiblings and so on)" (Condry 2001: 175). Texts comment on the problems of Japanese culture—the stress on seniority, for instance, worrying over the effects of the worst economic situation Japan has experienced since World War II with their fathers out of work and themselves unable to find a job, commenting on the problems of contemporary life, as in "Tokyo, Tokyo," by K-Dub Shine and DJ Kensei (CD track 35):

Series of skyscrapers
Losing faith in all the dramas happening there
The usual worries and patience are almost beyond limits
The year is Heisei 8 [1997]
In this sleepless city
Money moves in all the invisible places
The omens of this century
Still stalling. . . .
I'll find the other side of the river on my own
Change created by each individual
The direction of gaze one's choice
Reconsider the meaning of life
Cut my way through the golden days.
(Translation by Marié Abe)

K Dub Shine, the rapper on CD track 35, did experience hip-hop at its roots. Attending school in Oakland, California, he saw people clapping and rapping in school buses, rapping at cafeteria tables—just part of life. He wants to nurture the scene in Japan, to send clear messages to Japanese listeners. DJ Kensei, the DJ on CD track 35, worked his way to the top by winning international competitions.

ACTIVITY 5.2   *To gain a sense for yourself of the plethora of musical styles in global circulation that Japanese enjoy, surf the web for Japanese websites devoted to your favorite non-Japanese music and performers. You might be surprised at what you discover. Write a short report on what you searched for and what you did or did not find.*

CONTINUING THE INWARD LOOK

With rap as a transition, I segue now to the final portion of this chapter, in which I want to turn inward to look at moments of deep and meaningful fusion of ways of thinking and doing.

National Cultural Policies   In 1999 the composition partially reproduced as CD track 36 was premiered at the National Theater across the moat (and a street) from the Imperial Palace in Tokyo. Commissioned from the composer Keiko Fujiie, "Ten no yō na chi, soshite chi no yō na ten" ("Like heaven, earth so like earth, heaven") was among those in an ambitious program of fostering interest in traditional musics. The circumstances were these. Concerned by the potential loss of their traditional culture, in 1955 the government of Japan instituted an award system that accords national recognition to significant bearers of "Intangible Cultural Properties." Since then, numerous artists (from potters to dancers) have been designated as Living National Treasures. The *syakuhati* player Goro Yamaguchi (see pages 51–53) is an example.

Nevertheless, by the 1960s the full effects were being felt of the national endorsement of tonal music as the repertoire of choice for its public education system. You have read how that was reinforced by decades of commercial and artistic activity. When the generic term for music in Japanese language—*ongaku*—was assumed to refer to European classical (*kurasiku*) music, and music for traditional instruments (*hōgaku*) was as exotic to most Japanese as to non-Japanese (perhaps even more), something had to be done. In 1966, supported by government, the National Theater of Japan was founded with two aims: the preservation and the promotion of the traditional performing arts of the nation. Fully functioning until the present, the branches of the institution not only offer performances of traditional music and theater but also commission new works based on traditional styles of production and performance. They are fostering performing artists, composers, and the arts themselves.

Not surprisingly, given its history and status, *gagaku* is being featured prominently. From 1971 to 1999 the theater commissioned new pieces for *gagaku* instruments, causing a number of Japan's best composers who had no experience with traditional music to become involved.

One of those composers is Keiko Fujiie (b. 1963; figure 5.2). Discussing with me why she became attracted to *gagaku*, she made a good point: "The [cultural isolation of the] Edo period is a very great distance away. There is no way to approach it. But *gagaku* is somehow closer. It

FIGURE 5.2   *The composer Keiko Fujiie, 2000.   (Photo by the author.)*

came from so many places—Korea, China, India, etc. In ancient time, there was more contact with foreign people [as in present-day Japan]." Then she spoke about musical characteristics: "Pitch, for instance. It has certain [instrumental] pitch, whereas Edo music does not—the pitch always followed the human voice. And the sound of the *shō* is special; for me it was an entrance to approach the *gagaku* world. Also, *gagaku* has this idea of ensemble." When I asked Fujiie whether the structure of *gagaku* compositions was of interest to her, she replied: "*Gagaku* in the Heian period and now are so different that I don't know how to answer that. In the first half of the Heian period, there was so much improvisation" (personal communication, 4 June 2000).

Whereas some of the composers commissioned by the National Theater treated the *gagaku* ensemble quite like an orchestra—Toru Takemitsu, for instance, who wanted such a large group that amateur players had to be invited to join the Imperial Household musicians—Fujiie took the opportunity to learn about the ensemble as it functioned historically. Learning that in daily Heian elite life, there was constantly music making on the strings and winds without the percussion, she decided to follow suit in her piece.

ACTIVITY 5.3 *Listen closely to the portion of Fujiie's "Ten no yō na chi, soshite chi no yō na ten" (CD track 36) to analyze the following musical details. At 10:00 you will hear a fade out; the recording resumes just under three minutes later into the piece. As in traditional* gagaku *music, the* koto *and* biwa *can sometimes be difficult to tell apart. Generally listen for this: the* biwa *sounds lower, heavier, darker.*

Listen all the way through to answer each question. This is going to take you some time.

About the instruments:

• Plot the instrumentation of the piece from beginning to end. Which instrument begins? Which plays next? Note the timings, not only where instruments enter, but where they drop out.

• When and which instruments are scored together?

- Where are there "solo moments" when only one instrument type is heard?
- Is there a sense of flow or of form created through changing instrumentation? Even though I have made cuts in this long piece, you can gauge the flow of instrumentation.

About instrument parts and ensemble relationships:

- What is the musical nature of the *shō* part? Melody? Tonal clusters? Featured or accompanying?
- Does the *koto* play techniques you did not hear in "Etenraku" (CD track 10)?

About the melody:

- When the two string instrument types (*koto* and *biwa*) are being featured as a duo, what is their musical relationship? Partners, or one accompanying? Unison? Heterophony? Do you hear a tune? Do you hear any explicit melodic repetition?

About the rhythm:

- Do you hear breathing rhythm? Regular beats?
- Is there a sense of flow or of form created by the organization of time?

When you have answered all these analytical questions, review CD tracks 8, 9, and 10 and write an essay. The object of the essay is to compare Fujiie's use of the gagaku instruments with what you have previously heard. Has she referenced gagaku musical style in an intertextual manner, or has she used the instruments merely as instruments, without meaningfully connecting to gagaku music?

The Choral Phenomenon. It was no accident that early in Chapter 1 I referred to the annual singing of the choral finale of Beethoven's Symphony No. 9 (CD track 4), or that I chose to single out the men's chorus in *Men Who Step on the Tiger's Tail* (CD track 30). While there is no space in this textbook to elaborate on the subject, I want to acknowledge one of the most congenial developments from the interface with Western cultures—the deep love of singing together in choruses.

Enthusiasm for group singing is not new; no doubt it relates to the traditional practice of singing folk songs in unison in community festivities. The tonal nature of today's choral music, however, harks back to the harmonized songs sung in schools from the Meiji period, the Buddhist adoption of hymn singing from Christian missionaries, and the singing of hymns in the Christian schools to which many internationally minded, upwardly mobile Japanese families have sent their children. Choruses caught on and hundreds of thousands, if not millions, of Japanese sing in choruses, whether a children's chorus, teen chorus, mothers' chorus, young women's chorus, men's chorus, mixed chorus, PTA chorus, or business chorus. Composers in Tokyo insist that there are only two professional choruses in that huge metropolitan area, so most are amateur. Many choruses are casual, formed for social reasons more than musical, but many are musically serious and quite accomplished.

All types of choruses commission new music from contemporary composers. On the CD I have included three selections that exemplify the choral scene.

Distinguished Japanese composers are attracted to writing new music for young performers. "Chiisai aki mitsuketa" ("Found a small autumn," sung by a children's chorus on CD track 37) was composed by Yoshinao Nakada (1923–2000), one of the great songwriters of the twentieth century. Obviously meant for children, the first verse of "Chiisai aki" refers to a children's game in which "it" (*oni-san*) is blindfolded and chases others by hearing which direction the handclapping sounds come from.

Chiisai aki mitsuketa
Someone, someone, someone found
A small autumn, a small autumn,
found a small autumn.
Blindfolded oni-san, come to the sound of clapping hands
Subtly soaked in the ears which are keenly listening
are the whistling calls, the call of a butcher-bird.
A small autumn, a small autumn,
Found a small autumn. (Lyrics by Hachiro Sato, translation by Marié Abe)

I have found that many songs such as this that are composed for children are sung in performances by adults as well.

Commissioned for the Little Singers of Tokyo, one of the best children's choruses in the world, Toshio Hosokawa's "Singing Trees" (1997;

FIGURE 5.3 *The composer Toshio Hosokawa, 2000.   (Photo by the author.)*

CD track 38) is a difficult, sophisticated piece of music. While "Singing Trees" was still in its conception stage, Toru Takemitsu passed away, and Hosokawa (figure 5.3) wrote the piece as a requiem for him. (See more on Hosokawa below.)

Tokuhide Niimi (b. 1947; figure 5.4) has written a version of his Symphony No. 2 to include a chorus whose musical part has no text; as you can hear on CD track 39, Niimi has incorporated the voices into the orchestra. While attending Geidai, Niimi had the experience of singing in a chorus conducted by the distinguished freelance director Megumi O-naka. A serious commitment outside the university, it set a precedent for his career (Niimi, personal communication, 12 May 2001). Even while teaching at Toho Ongaku Daigaku and composing for major instrumental ensembles, Niimi remains committed to the choral world,

FIGURE 5.4   *The composer Tokuhide Niimi, 2002.   (Photo by the author.)*

writing interesting new music for all levels of expertise, from the "most amateur" of choruses to professional.

MUSIC AND THE MEDIA

The connections between music and the mass media in Japan are tight: film, TV, radio, and the recording industry are utterly intertwined. Relating how that happened, from the perspective of films, the historian of popular culture Mark Schilling has traced it in nutshell fashion, and I shall draw liberally from his account in the next sections (personal communication, 10 May 2001).

Film Music.   Music for film has changed radically through time. I noted earlier that the "classical music" composer Toru Takemitsu was known best in Japan for his many musical scores, particularly for films directed by Akira Kurosawa. Takemitsu was not unusual, however; until fairly recently writing music for film was one of the few steady sources of income for many composers. Especially famous examples are the score for *Seven Samurai* (a Kurosawa film) by Fumio Hayasaka,

Kwaidan by Takemitsu, and the incredibly successful series of Godzilla movies, with music by Akira Ifukube, one of the most important of all teachers of composition in twentieth-century Japan.

Samurai films, with *syamisen* music, were popular from the very beginning of Japanese cinema; silent swordplay films from 1910 were modeled on *kabuki* and shown with dramatic narration by a *bunraku*-like *benshi* who specialized in film stories. Japan's first sound film, *The Neighbor's Wife and Mine,* was about a jazz vocalist who moves next door. From before World War II and into the 1950s, the Japanese film industry produced Hollywood-type musicals with big stages, people singing on Ferris wheels, big dance numbers, and such. Much film music in those days consisted of American popular tunes, hit records of Latin numbers and show tunes, as well as *enka* sung by Misora Hibari, a great child star (CD track 40).

Into the 1960s, as such movies faded in the United States, in Japan they moved into TV format; there were many musical television shows. Gangster films of the 1960s featured "dreadful sentimental stuff"; as a good gangster wields his sword against twenty or thirty bad gangsters, an *enka*-like musical number would accompany his lonely meeting with fate. Until one producer, Shundo Koji, asserted the importance of music, the whole film would be made and a composer brought in at the very end. Koji began to dictate which music should be used, frequently turning to popular song hits, often sung by the actors. Singers were brought in to play the roles of lovers. Therein the foundation was laid for a close relationship between movies and pop stars—and between TV and pop stars. In the 1970s and 1980s "idol movies" (*idoru eiga*), a major subgenre, featured a model or a pop star from TV who had made a big recording hit. The idol just appeared, not necessarily doing anything.

Enka. A gradual process of popularization has taken place in the industry, resulting in a near loss of film music as a distinctive genre. The beginning of the process can be traced primarily to 1930s theme songs—slow, sentimental melodies with single-line accompaniment with which the modern *enka* began (Hosokawa, Matsumura, and Shiba 1991: 10–12). By the early 1970s the word *enka* came to be used by the media to describe a genre of popular Japanese music that filled a musical void for people not young enough to feel comfortable with rock and folk derivatives in Japan and who demanded their own music. *Enka* songs were usually a slow to medium-speed ballad, with texts (based on a 1920s model) expressing despairing sadness and self-sacrificing fatalism (Mitsui 1998: 39–40). In the early days of *karaoke* in Japan, *enka* comprised the repertory, appealing to middle-aged and elderly people who had literally devoted their lives to rebuilding the Japanese nation.

> To the Japanese public [now], *enka* sounds timelessly old, although it is still actively created and consumed. The erasure of passing time is in fact part of its attraction. A 1993 hit is deliberately contrived to be easily mistaken for a 1953 one . . . and for the duration of the song, the forty-year gap is neatly erased. What helps to achieve this time-lessness are not only the sounds and the images of *enka* but also—and most important—its sentiment. Here are hometowns left long ago but not forgotten, lovers parted, mothers remembered for their sacrifices. Amid the tumult and complexity of today's Japan, which faces chal-lenging questions of political leadership, economic recession, and globalization, these affairs of the heart, dredged up from a recon-structed past, seem wonderfully simple, direct, and untarnished. . . . Its reputation [is that of] "*nihon no uta*" (song of Japan), an expression of "*nihonjin no kokoro*" (the heart/soul of Japanese) and even "*dentō no oto*" (the sound of tradition). Amid the nationalistic cultural fervor of the 1970s, the record industry promoted *enka* as one emblem of na-tional culture. (Yano 2002: 3, 4)

The "Japaneseness" of *enka* is both visible and audible. Female singers still emphasize its "Japaneseness," dressed almost always in *kimono*. Al-though the *enka* accompaniment is chordal and is played on saxophones, trumpets, electric guitar, electric bass, piano, and strings, other musical traits identify it sonically as "Japanese." Older as well as recent songs are in pentatonic minor scales that are reminiscent of (but not the same as) the *in* scale (C D♭ E♭ F G A♭ C) of much traditional music; you can hear this on CD track 40. A quick ornamental sort of "catch" in the voice is used to evoke emotion, as well as the heavy vibrato used by Misora Hibari on CD track 40. As in traditional music, the text is the most im-portant element. Hibari's song, "Sakura no uta," laments that "I lost everything, how painful it is to be alive." Its last verse invokes the beloved symbol of the cherry tree:

> *By now you whom I loved so dearly*
> *might have already forgotten about me and be happy.*
> *Should we sleep without saying good night*
> *Under the kind, fragrant cherry tree*
> *Under the cherry tree.* (Translation by Marié Abe)

J-pop. From *enka* to J-pop in film was a logical progression. Unlike the American practice of plugging in music from the period depicted in the film (pop or otherwise), most of the music in Japanese film is current pop. Most important is a theme song; it might be part of the film or, more likely, intended to be played over the credits. The lyrics of the song may not have a direct relation to the film but sum up the "feeling" of the film. To the performers' delight, people sit through the credits just to hear it. At the press release for a new movie, the pop star who will sing the theme song appears along with the director.

To become that pop star, there was and is a standard route that demonstrates the links among the media. Females, but also some males, get a start by making commercials, singing the all-important musical theme. If noticed there, they are asked to appear in TV drama and perhaps record a TV show theme song (for some shows, but not all, the song changes every six weeks, unlike American show themes). Along the way somewhere they make a CD. By that route they get into film. It is a packaging phenomenon, entirely molded by the industry.

An alternative route to stardom is the amateur talent competition. Since the 1970s several star singers have emerged from televised singing contests for young people up to the low teens. All ten members of Morning Musume, the biggest pop group at the time of my conversation with Shilling, formed their group after being chosen as winners on the TV talent show "Asayan." This route to success was even the theme of a movie, *Hawaii e iku* (*Let's go to Hawaii*), in which the vocalist Mura Shigeru plays a failed *enka* singer who decides to try the talent contest route, wins, goes to Hawaii with her manager, and gets on a stage show with a real *enka* singer.

Most important among the TV competitions is the four-hour New Year's Eve one to which millions of Japanese stay riveted, waiting to see which established musicians have been invited to perform and who among the aspiring artists invited that year will rise to the top. In 2002, reflecting a rage for Okinawan pop-folk (CD track 41), the Boom, the group that started the rage, was featured, and most of the invited artists were Okinawan.

The label "J-pop" applies to the idol scene and encompasses boy groups and girl groups as well as individual stars. When I noted that most of the J-pop stars whom Shilling was naming were female, and that I had found most of the CDs of pop music in the stores to be featuring females, Shilling responded that the females are more successful because they are admired by women and men, whereas males do not tend to attract male fans. One exception is the group SMAP, whose various creative activities attract fans who are less gender-specific (CD track 42).

The female industry-created idol singer can be recognized stylistically by a youthful, sometimes even "little girl" voice with a relatively nasal quality. Song form and chord progressions are more or less standardized in this music. Among the new idols is Misia (CD track 43); her appeal, like others in the idol scene, is to the young in the "dance scene." The "Queen of J-Pop" is Utada Hikaru, whom you can hear on CD track 44. Mixing English and Japanese in the lyrics is quite common, as knowledge of English is a prestige factor. Since Hikaru grew up in the United States, it comes easily to her.

> *Distance*
> *We can start over.*
> *We can't be one.*
> *Wanna be with you now.*
> *Someday*
> *We'll be able to embrace the distance.*
> *We can start sooner.*
> *I still wanna be with you.*

(Translation by Marié Abe)

Theme Songs.   Because the marketing of theme songs in their own right is another activity of the industry, broadcast and recording of theme songs are important vehicles to stardom. A number of recording companies also own their own publishing companies, and collections of theme songs are widely available in music stores. CD track 41 comprises moments from "Kotonoha," a theme song of the NHK morning drama series "Manten" in 2002, performed by Hirose Chitose. The distinctive vocal ornamentation at the beginning identifies it as Okinawan pop, a subset of J-pop and a rage in the Japanese diaspora as well as in Japan. Its lyrics often invoke nature:

> *What is the color of the dawn sky that you are looking up at?*
> *Blue and cool—the color of the flower yet to be seen.*
> *What is the color of the midsummer wind that you don't know?*
> *Holding heat—the color of the flower that is bittersweet.*

(Translation by Marié Abe)

The importance of the theme song to composers and in Japanese popular musical culture in general is hard to overestimate. Among those writing themes songs is the *hichiriki* player Hideki Togi (see chapter 3), whose works range from a documentary film on the birth of Emperor Akihito's granddaughter (who might someday become empress after centuries of successive emperors) to the ending theme song for a Play Station 2. In the former the theme played on *hichiriki* and one four-second between-phrase motive on *koto* are the only intertextual musical references to the status of the imperial family, in a composition otherwise Western in orchestration, harmony, and phrase structure. Togi, a former Imperial Household musician and member of an illustrious family of *gagaku* musicians, was the logical choice to write the theme song. Perhaps you are familiar with the theme songs for the *animé* films *Princess Mononoke* and *Spirited Away*, composed by Hisaichi Yuzuru, who worked closely with the famous *animé* producer Hayao Miyazaki. I leave it to you to decide whether or not you hear rhetorical suggestions of "Japaneseness" in this widely distributed music.

The New York Nexus.   Yet another route to the top in the Japanese popular music scene is to make it big abroad, thereby drawing attention back home. The individuality this fosters makes any discussion of the scene very complex, and I can only hint at it here. The audience in New York is, on the one hand, Asian Americans among whom "Japaneseness" is hip (manifested by *sushi*, Japanese films, popular music, and such), and on the other a general audience who can know avant-garde Japanese artists through such media as John Zorn's New Japan Series on his Paddock label.

Shonen Knife was the first all-girl punk rock group to make it big abroad and sustain popularity (CD track 45). From Osaka, the three singers—Naoko Yamako (guitar), Michie Nakatani (bass), and Atsuko Yamano (percussion and keyboards)—formed the group in 1981, naming it Shonen ("boy") Knife to create a cute but dangerous feeling.

> *Riding on the Rocket*
> *I wanna ride on the rocket and go to Pluto.*
> *The space food is marshmallow, asparagus, ice cream.*
> *Let's take the blue-eyed cat too.*
> *Ikō, ikō, everybody let's go*
> *Ikō, ikō, everybody let's go.*
> *Ikō, ikō, everybody ikō.*

(Words and music by Naoko Yamano; translation by Marié Abe)

Having peaked in the mid-1990s and consistently appearing on the Top 40 charts is Dreams Come True (DCT), two of whose three members spend about half the year in New York. Their musical style is eclectic, experimenting with a wide range of sounds—reggae, Portuguese *fado*, and numerous others (CD track 46). Speaking to issues important universally, the lead singer, Miwa Yoshida, has become an idol for both younger and older women, as well as female and male college students. The lyrics are not easily translatable.

24/7
Virtual happiness is not enough.
In reality I can't say "I just want to take you with me!"
  I'm such a coward.
My heart is flying high, filling up the melody. I'm longing for you.

(Translation by Marié Abe).

Noise.   There is controversy surrounding "noise"—that it is not a pop music or, possibly, not music at all. For purposes of "orienting its trajectory in the circulation of the Japanese and United States underground music scenes," Novak considers "noise" an underground pop music. He further notes that "throughout the 1980s and early 1990s noise moved from a deeply underground practice . . . by a few individuals in Japan, to its current position as an internationally recognized musical form, practiced in diverse configurations by performers from many nationalities" (1999: 23, 22).

In the noise scene, the turnaround of groups is fast. These groups may not make it to the top of the commercial market, but their avantgarde sounds are likely to be "the Japanese sound" to musicians in the United States. I mention here just three groups who have persisted with notable success. Ruins has been around since 1986; the duo of Hisashi Sasaki (bass) and Tatsuya Yoshida make what is marketed as "schizophrenic avant-progressive rock" (CD track 47). Boredom's "maniacally extreme cacophony" is indebted to the 1970s Kraut-rock movement. This noise/psychedelia/experimental rock band has also been in existence since 1986 and is respected internationally (CD track 48). Finally, a few moments from a deconstructed theme song by the composer for *animé* Takeo Yamashita will demonstrate the intertextual process even in the noise scene. Noise/avant-garde artist Yoshihide Otomo plays "Sabu to ichi to torimono-hikae" from an *animé* set in the Tokugawa era. The sound of the Japanese instrument is an intertextual reference (CD track 49). Earlier in this book I commented on the aesthetic inclusion of nonmusical sounds in Japanese traditional music, so it should come as no surprise that Japanese musicians would be attracted to the use of technology for sonic ends—for noise music.

CHAPTER 6

From Japan Outward

∞

Whereas in most of this book I have been relating and commenting on the internationalization of Japan internally, in this last chapter I shall focus on significant examples of "Japan in the world." With *enka* and J-pop—both now distributed widely in other Asian countries with growing popularity—and noise as the transition, I shall now shift focus to other practices and genres and Japanese musicians whose depth of experience in the international music scene has made significant contributions outside the country.

JAPANESE DIASPORAS

Since the end of the nineteenth century, people of Japanese ancestry have settled in appreciable numbers in the United States, Brazil, Canada, Peru, and many other countries. The exchange between new and old countries has been important for music. Niche musics, jazz, and new popular musics flow among them. The extent to which traditional Japanese music has been cultivated abroad has varied with the circumstances, but it has definitely played a part in the maintenance of a sense of ethnic identity and socialization (Olsen 1983; Hosokawa 2000).

Vital to the sense of community in Hawaii and numerous other parts of the United States are the festivities of *o-bon*, the annual Buddhist ritual honoring the dead (analogous to the Catholic and Orthodox Christian All Saint's Day). Every summer, gatherings draw Buddhists, Japanese Americans, Okinawan Americans, and others, regardless of age, gender, or ethnicity. Fast but repetitive line and circle dances can be learned easily, and many people don summer cotton *ukata*s or *happi* coats to get in the spirit.

Karaoke.   *Karaoke* was a term used in the music industry after the advent of the tape recorder. It denoted an instrumental performance of a song recorded on reel-to-reel tape by the house orchestra of a recording company as an accompaniment to singers for their practice (Mitsui 1998: 40). *Karaoke* for amateur singers was born in the early 1970s in Japan. Not that it was the first instance of combining recorded and live music in Japanese music making; that had been happening for many years, for instance, in the summer *o-bon* festival dances throughout Japan, where live *taiko* drumming complements recorded dance music. Its birth is equated with the invention of a machine that permitted simultaneous use of playback and microphone and provided a device for the instantaneous selection of a song. That technology spawned an international sociomusical phenomenon, with Japanese manufacturers supplying the hardware. The "Japanese national obsession with singing along with technology" (Mitsui and Hosokawa 1998: 10) is now an international rage.

Jazz and "Japaneseness." In the late 1950s some Japanese jazz musicians revolted against the hegemony of American standards of aesthetic innovation and expressive authenticity by asserting in their music the sound of a Japanese cultural identity. Some Japanese bands performing overseas adopted musical fusion as a deliberate strategy for constructing distinctive musical identities. One way to do so was to combine Japanese and Western instruments. That was reinforced in the mid-1960s by some American fusion jazz musicians such as the clarinetist Tony Scott, who recorded a minor classic of improvised music for Verve Records, *Music for Zen Meditation and Other Joys*, with *syakuhati* player Hozan Yamamoto and *koto*ist Shinichi Yuize—both greats in the *hōgaku* world.

Jazzifying Japanese folk material was another way to accomplish this. The belief that Japanese bands were most likely to be successful overseas if they stuck to material that was identifiably "Japanese" (i.e., different) was more often than not confirmed by foreign audiences who expected originality, if not exoticism. "Jazzing" Japanese folk songs seemed to be a failsafe measure for deflecting accusations of excessive derivation from American sources (Atkins 2001: 243). For other Japanese musicians, however, originality was the goal, individual styles that were not necessarily rooted in nationality or ethnicity, and the interest in "Japaneseness" reached an apex in the late 1960s.

While the idea of a "national style" noticeably lost momentum in the 1970s, the work of two successful musicians, the percussionist Masahiko Togashi (who was inspired by Toru Takemitsu) and the pianist Toshiko Akiyoshi, kept the ideal of a Japanese style of jazz in circulation.

Akiyoshi studied at the Berklee School of Music in Boston, Massachusetts, and has made her career primarily in America and Europe. A composer-pianist, Akiyoshi by 1980 had become the "Triple Crown Queen," the first woman and the first non-American to win in three categories (big band, arranger, and composer) in any jazz poll (Atkins 2001: 259). Recording for big band with her husband, the tenor saxophonist and flutist Lew Tabackin, Akiyoshi is perhaps best known for her stirring composition "Kogun" ("Solitary Soldier," CD track 50). From the liner notes of her first album by the same name:

> It was October of 1972 when Japanese soldier, Second Lieutenant Hiroo Onoda, was discovered to be still alive, hiding and fighting alone in the jungle of a Philippine island without knowing about the defeat of Japan in World War II almost 30 years ago. Toshiko, who was impressed with Onoda's patriotic life, composed this piece to dedicate to him. . . . This is one of the most important works which reflects her attempt to express cultural traditions of Japan and Japanese sentiment through the vocabularies of the western art form of jazz. (translation by Marié Abe)

ACTIVITY 6.1 *In the brief excerpt from Toshiko Akiyoshi's "Kogun" on CD track 50) you should be able to hear two reminders of traditional Japanese music discussed in this book. Identify them.*

Gendai Ongaku.   The reaction of international audiences to Japanese jazz musicians—those who want to hear something rhetorically Japanese and therefore exotic—reminds me of what I have observed numerous times while doing field research on *gendai ongaku*, or contemporary classical music. Appearing in symposia or presenting guest talks about their pieces outside of Japan, Japanese composers who have been thoroughly educated in European classical music have each almost inevitably been asked, as if something were lacking: "What is Japanese about your music?"

I have found that the response of Japanese composers and musicians to international cultures differs from individual to individual. Some Japanese composers have told me that they first became self-conscious about "Japaneseness" in their music when confronted by that question, and it opened their eyes to indigenous musical traditions that they had little if any desire to experience previously. Some decide to explore it for purposes of composition, while others remain uninterested. Other composers with education in European music have cared deeply about expressing "Japaneseness" through their musical creativity and explored ways of doing that. In chapter 3 you read about Minoru Miki and Toru Takemitsu. All the composers discussed below have extensive experience with the international music scene.

Sharing the Concern about "Japaneseness."   The composer of "Singing Trees" (CD track 38), Toshio Hosokawa, was born in 1955 in Hiroshima. He pursued music studies initially in Japan but, like many other fine Japanese composers, studied composition abroad—with the Korean composer Isang Yun in Berlin, and with Klaus Huber and Brian Ferneyhough in Freiburg. He resides in both Japan and Germany. When I asked him why he lives in Germany, he replied that it is better and easier for Japanese composers to live and work in Europe, particularly in France and Germany. They get many commissions and performances, and "there are not so many bureaucratic obstacles" (personal communication, May 2001). Nevertheless, Hosokawa returns to Japan frequently to keep his musical connections there lively, and he is one of relatively few Japanese composers whose works are programmed by the Europe-oriented Japanese orchestras.

Program notes for Hosokawa compositions frequently mention his preoccupation with finding a true Japanese voice. This, for example, appeared in the notes for Fontec FOCD 3420, *Works by Toshio Hosokawa VI*:

Some 120 years ago, the people of Japan met up with what is called "western civilization," a great culture previously unknown to us. That encounter, however, was something that originated from outside Japan, not in response to our own inner prompting. The people of Japan felt pressed to assimilate into "western civilization," with the result that we turned our backs on our own origins. The participation of the Japanese people in world culture by assimilating into "western civilization" is a far cry from that adventure which began on Abraham's riverbank in Babylon, namely, the setting out into the unknown in response to one's own inner behest. And it has produced all sorts of psychological strains and moral dilemmas for us. As a Japanese living in the latter half of the 20th century, I am engaged in a search for a new music which is an adventure not in the spirit of assimilation. I am searching for a new form of spiritual culture and music of the Japanese people, which is at the same time true to my self and to my origins.

Expressing "Japaneseness" Aesthetically. Known in Japan mostly for collaborating with Akira Kurosawa to write voluminous amounts of music for film as well as for concerts, Toru Takemitsu was catapulted into international fame through "November Steps I" for orchestra, *biwa*, and *syakuhati*. Commissioned by the New York Philharmonic in celebration of its 125th anniversary in 1967, the premiere was guest-conducted by young Seiji Ozawa, then of the Toronto Symphony, whose fame as a conductor in international circles would come to match that of Takemitsu as composer. Perhaps the most intense interface of Japanese musicians with the international world of classical music has been through those two men, as both cultivated careers beyond Japan.

Asked to name one characteristic of Japanese music, listeners are likely to respond with "*ma.*" (see activity 3.1) This is due to Takemitsu—because he had discovered the aesthetic of time and space in traditional music, and because he wrote and spoke about it all over the world on a regular basis. Here is a sample from his writing:

October 6, [1961] Heard *gagaku* at the Imperial Household Agency. Certainly I was impressed by the ascending sounds that towered toward heaven like a tree. While the soundwaves of the music float through the air and by necessity exist in time, my impression of *gagaku* was that of a music that challenges measurable time. . . .

Gagaku lacks the concept of beat in Western terms. Of course, a certain rhythm is present, woven by specific percussion instruments—namely, *kakko, taiko*—and the *shō*. However, they serve only to embroider the gossamer curtain of intricate sound. . . . The most important instrument here is the *shō*. My impression of ascending sounds and the secret of immensurable metaphysical time seems to be based on the sound of this instrument. Sound on the *shō* is produced by inhaling and exhaling. The resultant sound, continuous and without attack, does not generate external beats, but awakens an internal latent rhythm. *Gagaku* reveals a strong Buddhist influence. In hearing the stream of sounds it is possible to imagine the concept of transitoriness but not necessarily that of lifelessness. . . . There is also something in the pauses in a Noh drama that has to do with eternity. . . . Listening to the *shō* I began to think of a basic creative approach to negative space. (Takemitsu 1995: 6–8)

"Negative space" takes us to *ma*, a perception of space and time in Japanese aesthetics:

> *Ma* might be translated as "*a between*," that is, *between* treated as a noun and not as a preposition. It is the time between events, the space between objects, the relationship between people, or that moment in a person's mind between thoughts. It is the white space in a pen-and-ink drawing, the pause between notes, or the moment in a *shite* dance in the last section of a *nō* play when all movement is frozen. . . . In other words, *ma* describes neither space nor time, but the tension in the silence and in the space surrounding sounds and objects. (Galliano 2002: 14)

ACTIVITY 6.2 *Listen again to CD track 12 of syakuhati music and also to CD track 11, a brief excerpt from "November Steps" for biwa, syakuhati, and orchestra, in which Takemitsu collaborated with distinguished Japanese artists. Keep in mind the description of* ma *as space and silence, and also the idea of there being no clear moment in which sound and silence begin and end. Try to identify moments when you think you hear this concept played out musically; note the timings in CD track 12 for discussions in class. No hearing is right or wrong; the experience of* ma *can be quite subjective.*

The composer Joji Yuasa (figure 6.1) is also deeply inspired aesthetically and intellectually by Japanese tradition. Born in 1929, Yuasa studied the chanting of the *nō* drama for several years as a boy. He was not headed for a career in music, however; he attended Keio University as a premedical student. Yuasa describes himself as a self-taught composer who stumbled into music as a club activity in college. He turned to music full-time in 1951, joining several young artists in a group that became significant in Japanese music—the Experimental Workshop.

Our conversation about his early musical activity led to his explanation of the emergence of the workshop:

> After World War II the French system was imported to Japan to replace the German system when Professor Ikenouchi at Geidai insisted,

FIGURE 6.1   *The composer Joji Yuasa with the author, 1999.   (Photo by Ann Pescatello.)*

"One must study Ravel until one masters his *'culture.'* " It was an emphasis on one historical European music over another. We, the members of the Experimental Workshop, had never composed "Sonata," while most other Japanese composers had. And we thought: We must have our own musical expression while studying European *contemporary* music of that time, namely, Schoenberg, Webern, Varèse, Messiaen, Jolivet, Stockhausen, Nono, Berio, etc. We did concerts and collaborated with artists in other fields. There were eleven members in all: five composers, four painters, one pianist, and one lighting expert, although there was no word like "intermedia" then. There were seven years of activity, to 1957. Then we each continued in our own way.

Significantly, four of the five composers, including Yuasa and Takemitsu, never went to music school (personal communication, May 2002).

Yuasa first came to the United States in 1968 on a six-month Japan Society fellowship that gave him the opportunity to visit a number of composition programs including those at Columbia University, Michigan, and Illinois. Keeping his international connections lively, in 1976 Yuasa received a Ford Foundation grant for residency at the Center for Experimental Music at UC San Diego, and he joined the faculty there in 1981. He has written for orchestra, chorus, chamber ensembles, electronics and computer, and for television, film, and theater. Having retired in 1994, he is Professor Emeritus of UC San Diego. Now living in Tokyo, Yuasa leads a busy life of teaching and composing.

In order to return to the theme of intertextuality through Yuasa's work, I have chosen to focus on one of his compositions, "Scenes from Basho" (1980) for orchestra (CD track 2). Perhaps you have heard of the great poet Matsuo Basho (1644–94) and of *haiku*, the condensed poetic form in which he wrote. Of the three independent movements of "Scenes from Basho," CD track 2 reproduces part of the second, which Yuasa based on this poem:

Blinding bright,
Relentless sun—
    But the wind is of autumn.
(Liner notes, Fontec FOCD 2508)

ACTIVITY 6.3   *Listen to CD track 2 with these musical details in mind: delicate instrumental colors, the ebb and flow of different musical layers that create a sense of immense spaces, and also the sense of the imagery in the poem, as well as the sense of the summer season turning into fall. Make a chronological timing chart of your impressions for class discussion.*

The Seasons in Japanese Music.   In Japanese tradition, an awareness of nature has shaped a good deal of aesthetic expression, often in the form of thematic intertextuality. Recurring again and again in art, poetry, and music from ancient times to the present are motifs of nature, among them wind, water, birds, trees, blossoms—and also the seasons, each with meaningful connotations. I think of some traditional gardens in Japan, designed and planted so that they will be transformed and distinctively beautiful in each season. In the plum blossoms pictured in paintings and other forms of art every Japanese recognizes the reference to the first tree to blossom in spring—representing strength, however delicately. To picture a vivid red-orange persimmon prolongs the memory of the nostalgia of autumn.

While I have not made a point of it until now, selections on this book's CD reflect this intertextual referencing of the seasons: for summer and autumn, Yuasa's "Scenes from Basho" (CD track 2) and Nakada's "Chiisai aki mitsuketa" (CD track 37); for winter the *gagaku* mode *banshiki* (CD tracks 8 and 10) and the February setting of *Ataka, Kanjinchō,* and *Men Who Step on the Tiger's Tail;* for spring, Michio Miyagi's "Haru no umi" (CD track 20), evoking the ocean in spring, and Misora Hibari's *enka* "Sakura no uta," "Song of the Cherry Blossoms" (CD track 40). I cannot resist at least mentioning the popular music band the Tube, which performs only in summer, with songs on the theme of that season.

And, you might remember, I mentioned that Vivaldi's "Four Seasons" holds a favored spot among compositions of European classical music (CD track 1, "Summer"). After the four concertos in the set had already been conceived, the Italian composer Vivaldi had poems printed along with the musical parts to describe each of the seasons. Due to the centuries long practice of intertextuality in their culture, it is not surprising to me at all that such a work, uniting poetry and music and the seasons, would be adopted by Japanese music lovers.

Keiko Abe and the Marimba. Finally, with the seasons on our minds, I turn to Keiko Abe (figure 6.2) through her composition for marimba "Dream of the Cherry Blossoms" (CD track 51) in which she invokes that quintessential image of spring. "After full bloom, the petals of the cherry blossoms are blown away from the tree creating a blizzard by gusts of the spring breeze. This work recreates this unique atmosphere in a subtle yet profound manner" (liner notes of Xebec XECC-1004). If you listen closely, you can perhaps hear that one pitch (E) is centrally integrated and is always played in the same tempo. The melody of the beloved Japanese folksong "Sakura" is fragmented and, although represented in many variations, is always clear.

Born in Tokyo in 1937 to a doctor father and artist mother, Abe attended a mission school for junior high school, and there at age twelve

FIGURE 6.2 *The virtuoso marimba player and composer Keiko Abe, 2001. (Photo by the author.)*

encountered the missionary Lawrence Lacour, who "brought marimba to Japan" (Abe, personal communication, 11 May 2001). There was a straight line from that time to her career as a performer and composer. Attending Tokyo Gakugei University in music education, she graduated with an M.A. at age twenty-two, still playing percussion. Abe credits the composer Isao Tomita (associated with synthesizer music) for getting her started as a professional performer; he needed a percussionist who could make organ sounds on a marimba. Since Lacour had played hymns on marimba, that was no problem for her.

Keiko Abe, however, wanted to turn the marimba from "just a part of percussion" into a solo instrument. She commissioned pieces at first, and her career was really launched with an award-winning LP in 1968. Interested in improvising, she went to America in 1977 to find musicians; in the meantime her playing and, from 1971, her own compositions were beginning to attract a following in Japan. To really "make it big," Abe decided to commission pieces from the best Japanese contemporary composers. Among them was Minoru Miki, who, after hearing her play the concerto she commissioned from him, remarked to her that the American marimba she was using did not fit her musicality. "You need to develop it more," she reports his having said. (This type of encouragement should sound familiar from the discussion of Keiko Nosaka and her creation of the twenty-stringed *koto* in chapter 3.) So Abe asked the Yamaha company to help; Yamaha "gave me an engineer to work with," she said modestly. The last result was a five-octave marimba with a deep sound (Yamaha Marimba YM-6000). With it her career skyrocketed; she has toured North America, Europe, and Asia repeatedly, recorded many CDs, and was the first woman inducted into the Percussive Arts Society Hall of Fame. On 1 November 2001, from Grand Rapids, Michigan, Yamaha announced a Keiko Abe signature set of mallets. Abe's artistry, her creativity, and her technological innovations are among Japan's gifts to the international community in music.

CONCLUSION

In this chapter the book's three themes come full circle. The interface of Japan with other cultures continues unabated, with Japan participating in the give and take that is characteristic of today's global world. Likewise, the intertextual process continues to be vital. In the creative output of artists in multiple performance genres and scenes, references are being made to shared understandings in terms material, musical, textual, and aesthetic. As well, the gradual process of popularization that has occurred throughout the centuries continues, if not accelerates, into the twenty-first century in forms as diverse as *animé* and noise. Japan's vibrant assimilative culture, the juxtaposition of popular and classical, and the process of internationalization along with reflection by the Japanese on "Japaneseness" result in a unique and significant practice: Japanese music.

Glossary

∞

Aerophone Instruments whose primary sound-producing medium is vibrating air

Aragoto Exxagerated male acting style in *kabuki*

Au "Matched," congruent rhythm between vocal part and drums in *nō*

Awazu "Nonmatched," incongruent rhythm between vocal part and drums in *nō*

Bandoya Band for hire

Banshiki-chō One of six melodic modes in imperial court music

Biwa Short-necked, ovoid-shaped plucked lute

Bugaku Dances and dance pieces of the imperial court music repertoire

Bunraku Puppet theater

Chang-gu Double-headed, hourglass-shaped drum in Korean music

Chirashi Section of a *nagauta* piece

Chō (chōshi) Melodic mode

Chōshi Long prelude in imperial court music

Chordophone Instrument whose primary sound-producing medium is a vibrating string

Colotomic structure Articulation of the metric grouping by one or more instruments in a Southeast Asian ensemble

Dan Section of a play or musical composition

Dangire Section of a *nagauta* piece

Enka Nostalgic popular song genre

Fue   Generically, flute

Fushi   Melody in *nō* drama style

Gagaku   Music of the Imperial court and Buddhist temples

Gaikyoku   Pieces in the *syakuhati* repertoire other than *honkyoku*

Geidai   Abbreviation for Tokyo National University of Fine Arts and Music

Geza   Side-stage instrument room for *kabuki* plays

Hanamichi   Visible walkway onto the stage in *kabuki*

Hayashi   Instrumental ensemble

Hyōshi   Beat, or metric structure

Haya yo hyōshi   Metric structure of four measures of four beats each

Heterophony   One melody performed in slightly different versions simultaneously

Hōgaku   Traditional music, or "traditional" music for Japanese instruments

Honkyoku   Fundamental pieces in a repertoire

Hyōjo   One of six melodic modes in imperial court music

Idiophone   Instrument whose vibrating body is the primary sound- producing medium

Iemoto   Head of a group of practitioners in the *iemoto seito*

Iemoto seito   Traditional system for transmission of knowledge

Jiuta   Pieces by blind *syamisen* players of the Kansai region

Jo-ha-kyu   Aesthetic structure

J-pop   Popular music by Japanese musicians

Kabuki   Seventeenth-century theatrical form

Kakegoe   Cueing calls of drummers and *syamisen* players

Kakko   Double-headed barrel drum in *tōgaku ensemble*

Kangen   Instrumental ensemble music of imperial court music

Kansai   Western region of Honshu Island

Kantō   Eastern region of Honshu Island

Katakana   Japanese script for writing foreign words

Kokata   Role of a child in a *nō* play

Komabue   Transverse flute used in *komagaku* ensemble

Komagaku   Pieces of imperial court music that were imported from Korea and Manchuria

Komusō   *Syakuhati*-playing Fuke Zen sect priests in Tokugawa era

Koto   Plucked long zither (in *gagaku, sō no koto*)

Kotoba   "Words," heightened speech style in *nō*

Ko-tsuzumi   Waisted-shaped shoulder drum in *nō* ensemble

Kumi daiko   Any collection of drums and other percussion instruments for an ensemble

Kuri   Type of subsection in *nō* performance style

Kyōgen   Comic plays; character type in *nō* plays

Ma   A perception of space and time, a "between"

Matsuri bayashi   Ensemble music for festivals

Membranophone   Instrument whose primary sound producing medium is a vibrating membrane

Mie   Striking pose held for dramatic effect by *kabuki* actor

Nagauta   *Syamisen*-accompanied musical genre for *kabuki* and concert

Netori   Short prelude in imperial court music

NHK   Nihon Hoso Kyokai (Japan Broadcasting Company)

Nō   Fifteenth-century music drama of the *samurai* class

Nōkan   Horizontal bamboo flute in *nō*

Noriji   Type of subsection in *nō* performance style

Nukui-bayashi   One style of *Matsuri bayashi* of Meguro district, Tokyo

Ongaku   Generically, "music"

O-mikoshi   Portable shrine

Onnagata   Actor playing female role in *kabuki*

Ō-tsuzumi   Waisted-shaped hip drum in *nō ensemble*

Rōnin   Masterless *samurai*

Ryū   Traditional teaching group; school

Sageuta   Type of subsection in *nō* performance style

Sake   Rice wine

Samurai   Warrior; military class in premodern Japan

San-hsien   Chinese predecessor of *syamisen*

Sankyoku   Three instruments playing a piece together

San no tsuzumi   Double-headed hourglass shaped drum in *komagaku* ensemble

Sensei   Teacher

Seiyō   Western style

Shidai   Instrumental entry music and initial song in *nō* plays

Shite   Principle character role in a *nō* play

Shō   Mouth organ in imperial court music ensemble

Shōdan   Subsection of a *nō* play

Shōgun   Head of the military *samurai* government

Shōko   Gong in imperial court music ensemble

Sō no koto   Long zither in imperial court music ensemble

Syamisen (shamisen)   Plucked long-necked lute

Syakuhati (shakuhachi)   Vertical bamboo flute

Taiko   "Drum"; frame drum in *gagaku*; barrel-shaped drum in *nō* ensemble

Tatami   Straw-mat flooring

Tōgaku   Pieces of imperial court music from in and south and west of China

Tokiwazu   *Syamisen*-accompanied musical genre for *kabuki* and concert

Tokonoma   Niche in Japanese room for display of treasured items

Tsugaru *jamisen (syamisen)*   Style of music for voice and *syamisen* from northern Honshu Island

Tsure   Supporting character role in a *nō* play

Tsuyogin   Chantlike dynamic singing style in *nō*

Ukiyo-e   Woodblock prints depicting the "floating world" of pleasure in Tokugawa-period Japan (1600–1868)

Waki   Second principle character role in a *nō* play

Wayō   Indigenous (Japanese) style

Yowagin   Truly melodic singing in *nō*

References

∞

Atkins, E. Taylor. 2001. *Blue Nippon: Authenticating Jazz in Japan*. Durham, N.C.: Duke University Press.

Baerwald, Hans H. 2002. "Postwar Japan: A Reminiscence." *Bulletin* (International House of Japan) 22.1 (spring): 30–47.

Blasdel, Christopher Yohmei. 1990. *Shakuhachi oddesei-ten no neiro ni miserarete* (*Searching the Single Tone: A Personal Journey into Japanese Music*) (English translation by the author). Tokyo: Kawade Shobo Shinsha.

Cahoon, Keith. 1993. "Popular Music in Japan." In *Japan: An Illustrated Encyclopedia*, 1287. Tokyo: Kodansha.

Condry, Ian. 2000. "The Social Production of Difference: Imitation and Authenticity in Japanese Rap Music." In *Transactions, Transgressions, and Transformations*, ed. Heide Fehrenbach and Uta G. Poiger, 166–84. New York: Berghan Books.

———. 2001. "A History of Japanese Hip-Hop: Street Dance, Club Scene, Pop Market." In *Global Noise: Rap and Hip-Hop Outside the USA*, ed. Toni Mitchell, 222–47. Middletown, Conn.: Wesleyan University Press.

De Ferranti, Hugh. 2000. *Japanese Musical Instruments*. New York: Oxford University Press.

De Marinis, Marco. 1993. *The Semiotics of Performance*. Trans. Aine O'Healy. Bloomington: Indiana University Press.

Eppstein, Ury. 1994. *The Beginnings of Western Music in Meiji Era Japan*. Lewiston, N.Y.: Edwin Mellen Press.

Fairbank, John K., Edwin O. Reischauer, and Albert M. Craig. 1973. *East Asia: Tradition and Transformation*. Boston: Houghton Mifflin.

Fujitani, T. 1996. *Splendid Monarchy: Power and Pageantry in Modern Japan*. Berkeley and Los Angeles: University of California Press.

Galliano, Luciana. 2002. *Yōgaku: Japanese Music in the Twentieth Century*. Trans. Martin Mayes. Lanham, Md.: Scarecrow Press.

Gold, Lisa. 2005. *Music in Bali: Experiencing Music, Expressing Culture*. New York: Oxford University Press.

Harich-Schneider, Eta. 1954. *The Rhythmical Patterns in Gagaku and Bugaku.* Leiden: Brill.

Herd, Judith Ann. 1987. "Change and Continuity in Contemporary Japanese Music: A Search for a National Identity." Ph.D. diss. Brown University.

Hosokawa, Shuhei. 1999. " 'Salsa no tiene frontera': Orquesta de la Luz and the Globalization of Popular Music." *Cultural Studies* 3.3: 509–34.

Hosokawa, Shuhei. 2000. "Singing Contests in the Ethnic Enclosure of the Post-War Japanese-Brazilian Community." *Brazilian Musics, Brazilian Identities*, special issue of the *British Journal of Ethnomusicology* 9.1: 95–118.

Inoue, Keiichi, Eriko Ozawa, Tadahiro Sakon, and Mie Hosaka. 1996. *Talking about Japan: Q & A.* Tokyo: Kodansha International.

Ivy, Marilyn. 1995. *Discourses of the Vanishing: Modernity, Phantasm, Japan.* Chicago: University of Chicago Press.

Japanese Classics Translation Committee, trans. 1960. *Ataka.* In *Japanese Noh Drama* 3:149–72. Tokyo: Nippon Gakujutsu Shinkokai.

Kawakami, Genichi. 1987. *Reflections on Music Popularization.* Tokyo: Yamaha Music Foundation.

Kitahara Ikuya, Misao Matsumoto, Akira Matsuda. 1990. *The Encyclopedia of Musical Instruments: The Shakuhachi.* Supervised by Tanimura Ko and Kōzō Kitahara. Tokyo: Tokyo Ongakusha.

Malm, William. 1983. "Japanese Music and its Relations to Other Musical Traditions." *World of Music* 25.1: 5–15.

May, Elizabeth. 1959. "Japanese Children's Folk Songs before and after Contact with the West." *Journal of the International Folk Music Council* 11: 59–65.

————. 1963. *The Influence of the Meiji Period on Japanese Children's Music.* Berkeley and Los Angeles: University of California Press, 1963.

Mitsui, Toru. 1998. "The Genesis of Karaoke: How the Combination of Technology and Music Evolved." In *Karaoke around the World*, ed. Toru Mitsui and Shuhei Hosokawa, 31–44. New York: Routledge.

Mitsui, Toru and Shuhei Hosokawa, eds. 1998. *Karaoke Around the World.* New York: Routledge.

Novak, David. 1999. "The National and the Transnational in the Japanese Underground." Master's thesis. Wesleyan University.

Olsen, Dale. 1983."The Social Determinants of Japanese Musical Life in Peru and Brazil." *Ethnomusicology* 27.1 (January): 49–70.

Sanford, James H. 1977. "*Shakuhachi* Zen: The *Fukeshû* and *Komusō.*" *Monumenta Nipponica* 32: 411–40.

Scott, A. C. 1953 *Kanjincho: A Japanese Kabuki Play.* Tokyo: Hokuseido Press.

Shively, Donald. 1955. "Bakufu versus Kabuki." *Harvard Journal of Asiatic Studies* 18: 326–56. Reprinted in John W. Hall and Marius B. Jansen, eds.,

Studies in the Institutional History of Early Modern Japan, 231–61. Princeton, N.J.: Princeton University Press, 1968.

———. 1978. "The Social Environment of Tokugawa Kabuki." In *Studies in Kabuki: Its Acting, Music, and Historical Context*. ed. James P. Brandon, William P. Malm, and Donald H. Shively, 1–61. Honolulu: University Press of Hawai'i.

Takemitsu, Toru. 1995. *Confronting Silence: Selected Writings*. Transl. and ed. Yoshiko Kakudo and Glenn Glasow. Berkeley, Calif.: Fallen Leaf Press.

Tanabe, Hideo and Genjiro Masu. 1953. *Japanese Music, the Japanese History of Customes [sic] through Music*. Tokyo: UnescoNippon.

Torikai, Shin-ichi. 2002. "Music and Dance to Welcome the Gods: *Nukui-bayashi*." *Nipponia* 22:18.

Tsuchiya, Komei. 2002 "These Two *Tsugaru-jamisen* Players Are Second to None: The Yoshida Kyodai." *Nipponia* 22:3.

Wade, Bonnie. 1994. "Keiko Nosaka and the Twenty-Stringed *Koto*: Tradition and Modernization in Japanese Music." In *The Musicological Juncture: Essays in Honor of Rulan Chao Pian*, ed. Bell Yung and Joseph S. C. Lam, 184–98. Cambridge, Mass: Harvard University Press.

———. 2000. "Negotiating the Future: Japanese Music as Case in Point." *Tongyang Umak* (Journal of the Asian Music Research Institute, Seoul National University) 22:1–18.

———. 2004. *Thinking Musically: Experiencing Music, Expressing Culture*. New York: Oxford University Press.

Yano, Christine R. 2002. *Tears of Longing: Nostalgia and the Nation in Japanese Popular Song*. Cambridge: Harvard University Asia Center, distributed by Harvard University Press.

Resources

∞

Print Sources

Bethe, Monica, and Richard Emmert. 1992. *Noh Performance Guides*. 7 vols. 1. *Matsukaze*. 5. *Atsumori*. Tokyo: National Noh Theater. Distributed by the Noh Training Project, Bloomsbury, Pa, c/o Learning Tomorrow, 53 West Main St., Bloomsbury, PA 17815. ⟨ntp@csrlink.net⟩.

Brandon, James R., and Tamako Niwa, adapt. 1966. *Kanjincho*. In *Kabuki Plays "Kanjincho" "The Zen Substitute,"* 1–48. New York: Samuel French.

Brandon, James R., with William P. Malm. 1978. *Studies in Kabuki: Its Acting, Music, and Historical Context*. Honolulu: University of Hawaii Press.

Brazell, Karen, ed. 1998. *Traditional Japanese Theater: An Anthology of Plays*. New York: Columbia University Press.

Fallows, James. 1994. "After Centuries of Japanese Isolation, a Fateful Meeting of East and West." *Smithsonian Magazine* 25.4 (July): 20, 21–24, 26–28, 30, 32–33.

Garfias, Robert. 1975. *Music of a Thousand Autumns: The Tōgaku Style of Japanese Court Music*. Berkeley and Los Angeles: University of California Press.

Hosokawa, Shuhei, Hiroshi Matsusmura, and Shun'ichi Shiba, eds. 1991. *A Guide to Popular Music in Japan*. Tokyo: IASPM-Japan/Ongakusha.

Gerstle, C. Andrew, Jiyoshi Inobe, and William P. Malm. 1990. *Theater as Music: The Bunraku Play "Mt. Imo and Mt. Se: An Exemplary Tale of Womanly Virtue."* Ann Arbor: Center for Japanese Studies, University of Michigan.

Kitahara, Michio. 1966. "*Kayokyoku*: An Example of Syncretism Involving Scale and Mode." *Ethnomusicology* 10.3:271–84.

Komparu, Kunio. 1983. *The Noh Theater: Principles and Perspectives*. New York: Weatherhill.

Malm, William P. 2000(a). *Japanese Music and Musical Instruments*. Tokyo: Kodansha International.

———. 2000(b). *Nagauta: The Heart of Kabuki Music*. Tokyo: Tuttle.

McCullough, Helen Craig, trans. 1988. *The Tale of the Heike*. Stanford, Calif.: Stanford University Press.

———. 1990 [1971]. *Yoshitsune: A Fifteenth-Century Japanese Chronicle.* Stanford, Calif.: Stanford University Press. See chapter 7 for details related to *Ataka/Kanjincho/Men Who Step on the Tiger's Tail.*

Mitchell, Toni, ed. *Global Noise: Rap and Hip-hop outside the USA.* Middletown, Conn.: Wesleyan University Press.

Peluse, Michael S. 2002. Folk Revival or Pop Sensation?: The Latest Tsugaru Shamisen Boom. MA thesis, Wesleyan University.

Provine, Robert C., Yosihiko Tokumaru, and J. Lawrence Witzleben, eds. 2002. *The Garland Encyclopedia of World Music.* Vol. 7. *East Asia: China, Japan, and Korea.* New York: Garland.

Read, Cathleen B., and David L. Locke. 1983. "An Analysis of the Yamada-ryū Sōkyoku [*koto*] Iemoto System." *Hōgaku* 1.1:20–52.

Savigliano, Marta E. 1995. "Exotic Encounters." In *Tango and the Political Economy of Passion*, 169–206. Boulder, Colo.: Westview Press.

Schilling, Mark. 1997. *The Encyclopedia of Japanese Pop Culture.* New York: Weatherhill.

Treat, John Whittier. 1996. *Contemporary Japan and Popular Culture.* Honolulu: University of Hawai'i Press.

Tyler, Royall, ed. & trans. 1992. *Japanese Nō Dramas.* London: Penguin Books.

Wade, Bonnie. 1976. *Tegotomono: Music for the Japanese Koto.* Westport, Conn.: Greenwood Press.

Yasuda, Kenneth. 1989 *Ataka.* In *Masterworks of the Nō Theater.* Bloomington: Indiana University Press.

Videography

Films for the Humanities and Sciences ⟨www.films.com⟩. This is a good source for educational videos on Japanese culture and history specifically relating to music and theater discussed in this textbook.

Bunraku: Masters of Japanese Puppet Theater. 52 minutes. HAN 30081. *Kabuki.* 35 minutes. HAN 1559.

Koto: The Music of Tadao. 48 minutes. HAN 30229. Features a composer and player of contemporary *koto* music.

Portrait of an Onnagata. Films for the Humanities and Sciences FFH 3802. 1995. 30 min. VHS. Reviews history, staging, and training for *kabuki.*

Shozan tanabe: The Sound of Silence. 47 minutes. HAN 30227. On *syakuhati* music.

Tsugaru shamisen: The World of Michihiro Sato. 48 minutes. HAN 30226.

Early Music Television. University of Oklahoma ⟨www.ou.edu/early music⟩. Specifically related to music and theatrical forms discussed in this textbook is an excellent Japanese music series produced by Eugene Enrico. Each video is narrated by William P. Malm and Sidney D. Brown.

Gagaku: The Court Music of Japan. 1989. History, instruments, dance, musical form, and a performance of *Etenraku.*

Jazz in Japan. 1999.

Music of Bunraku. 1991. Relates to the puppet theater.

Nagauta: The Heart of Kabuki Music. 1993. Explains the form of *nagauta* composition as performed in concert rather than in theater. The *dangire* and *chirashi* section of the piece is the same as that in *Kanjincho.*

Shinto Festival Music. 1993. Relates to *matsuri bayashi.*

Special Note: A video of Kanjincho will be released by NHK in late 2004. It could possibly be available through Bunkado (see this section) or through Kinokuniya, particularly its New York bookstore: 10 West 49th Street, NY, NY 10020. Tel: 212/765-7766; Fax: 212/541-9335.

Also, in late 2005-early 2006, a DVD is projected for release by the Criterion Collection (website: www.Criterionco.com). It will include Kurosawa's *Men Who Step on the Tiger's Tail,* with English subtitles and an English commentary track by Donald Ritchie. Complementary tracks will show video clips from Ataka and Kanjincho, including scenes discussed in this book. It will be distributed in North America by Marty Gross Productions, Inc. (website: www.Martygrossfilms.com).

Other Films and Videos

Jazz Is My Native Language: A Portrait of Toshiko Akiyoshi. Renee Cho, dir. Rhapsody Films, 1983. VHS

Men Who Step on the Tiger's Tail. 60 min. Akira Kurosawa, dir. Available from Amazon.com with English subtitles. Search also for *Men Who Tread. . .*

Noh Drama. New York: Japanese Information Center. 1984.

Tokyo Blues: Jazz and Blues in Japan. Craig McTurk, dir. 1999.

The Tradition of Performing Arts in Japan: The Artistry of Kabuki, Noh, and Bunraku. In the series *Japan: the Land and Its People.* Produced by Shin-Ei, Inc. 1989. VHS. 29 min. Distributed by GPN, P.O. Box 80669. Lincoln, NE 68501-0669 ⟨gpn@unlinfo.unl.edu⟩. The *kabuki* is the innovative *supakabuki* style.

Togi, Hideki. *Togi Hideki Concert.* Toshiba-EMI TOVF-1343. VHS. 2000.

The Ondeko-za on sado (Sadonokuni Ondeko-za). Masahiro Shinoda, dir. 1975. 57 min. Documentary.

Recording companies (see also CD list). Traditional music, unless noted
Camerata (contemporary composition)
    Camerata Tokyo, Inc.
    Wako Building, 2nd Floor, 14-3
    Tokyo, 151-0062 JAPAN
    Fax: (+81) 3-5790–5566
    Tel: (+81) 3-5790–5562
Celestial Harmonies
    4549 E. Fort Lowell Road
    Tucson, AZ 85712
    Toll free fax: 1/888/854-5898
    ⟨www.harmonies.com⟩
Denon
Fontec (contemporary composition)
    ⟨http://fontec.co.jp⟩
King Records
    King Record Co., Ltd.
    1-2-3 Otowa, Bunkyoku
    Tokyo, 112-0013 JAPAN
    ⟨http://www.kingrecords.co.jp⟩
Lyrichord
Nonesuch
Ocora

Other
Bunkado Record Shop: a major source for Japanese recordings and videos.
    14-1, 5-chome, Ginza
    Chuo-ku, Tokyo, JAPAN
    104-0061
Japan Society: a major contact for information about performing arts and
    recordings and videos in the United States.
    333 East 47th Street
    New York, New York 10017
    ⟨www.japansociety.org⟩

Index

∞